Also by PAUL KALAS

The Oneironauts: Using dreams to engineer our future

Crete Swim

An insider's guide to sightseeing

from the water

PAUL KALAS, PH.D.

NEW TERRA
PRESS

Copyright © 2021 by Paul Kalas
Updated March 2025

ALL RIGHTS RESERVED

Visit the book's web site at: www.creteswim.com

For information about permission to reproduce selections from this book, write to creteswim@gmail.com

Cover design: Aspasia Gkika and Paul Kalas
Figure and image credits: Paul Kalas
Satellite imagery: U.S. National Oceanic and Atmospheric Administration
Quotes from Homer: The Odyssey, translated by A.T. Murray, Ph.D. in two volumes. Cambridge, MA., Harvard University Press; London, William Heinemann, Ltd. 1919
Minoan artifacts: Heraklion Archaeological Museum

Without limiting the rights under copyright reserved above, no part of this publication may be reproduced, stored in or introduced into a retrieval system or transmitted, in any form, or by any means (electronic, mechanical, photocopying, recording, or otherwise), without the prior written permission of both the copyright owner and publisher.

The scanning, uploading, and distribution of this book via the Internet or any other means without the permission of the publisher is illegal. Please purchase only authorized editions and do not participate in electronic piracy of copyrightable materials. Your support of the author's rights is appreciated.

While the author has made every effort to provide accurate attributions and Internet addresses at the time of publication, neither the publisher nor the author assumes any responsibility for errors, or for changes that occur after publication. Further, the publisher does not have any control over and does not assume any responsibility for author or third-party Web sites or their content.

ISBN 979-1-7324631-8-9 (paperback color edition)
ISBN 978-1-7324631-9-6 (ebook)

New Terra Press
Berkeley, CA 94720
USA

To Aspa, Nikoleta, and Natalia

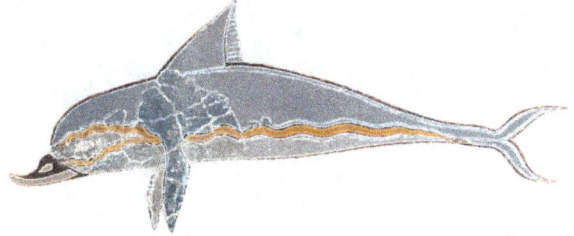

Contents

Preface .... **i**

1 Introduction **1**
   Orientation on Crete 3
   Swimming for Sightseeing 5
   Marine Navigation 7
   Weather Conditions (June–September) 20

2 The Basics: Safety, Gear & Preparation **27**
   Safety Tips 28
   Gear 42
   Preparation 49

3 North Coast of Crete **67**
   #1 Balos-Gramvousa 68
   #2 Marathi Island 70
   #3 Kamari Gastroswim 72
   #4 Spilies Tunnel and Sea Arch 73
   #5 Bali (the one in Crete) 75
   #6 The Green Coast – Agia Pelagia 76
   #7 Paleokastro Caves 79
   #8 Knossos Final Approach 80
   #9 Hersonissos Coves 84
   #10 Artemisia's Swim – Plaka to Spinalonga 85
   #11 Mochlos Island and Richtis Waterfall 89
   #12 Vai Palm Beach 91

4 South Coast of Crete **93**
#13 Xerokambos Falcon Islands 93
#14 The Galactic Night Swim 95
#15 Treis Ekklisies Caves 101
#16 Agiofaraggo 106
#17 Matala's Hidden Sea Caves 108
#18 Agios Pavlos Full Moon Swim 110
#19 The Amazing Gorge Swims 113
#20 Sfakia, Ilingas, Sweet Water, Loutro, Marmara, Talos 115
#21 Elafonisi Eye Candy 123

5 Other Beaches, Satellite Islands & Day Trips **125**

6 Crete Open Water Swim Competitions **133**

Glossary **137**

Disclaimer **140**

Index **141**

About the Author **145**

Preface

This is an updated edition of my guidebook for both recreational and competitive swimmers seeking fun adventure swimming at 30 locations around the fantastic Mediterranean island of Crete. Stand-up paddlers, snorkelers, and kayakers will enjoy my coastal tours as well.

The first half of the book includes an introductory guide to open water swimming to help those who are relatively new to this increasingly popular pastime. For experienced swimmers, this guide will expand their knowledge of safety and marine navigation. Even if you are not visiting Crete, you will become a better open water swimmer after reading this material.

In the second half of the book, some of my open water swims are as short as 50 meters roundtrip while other routes are up to 13 kilometers. All have been selected for their beauty, novelty, and history with local safety tips throughout. For those accompanying a swimmer friend or relative, rest assured that the beaches you'll be visiting are among the most spectacular on the island.

Though you will be hearing my voice as you read, what you really encounter is a Greek chorus of contributions from the people who live on Crete. My cousin Mijailos Nathenas has been my enthusiastic swim buddy for countless swims, providing seemingly endless tips on new places to explore. My daughters Nikoleta and Natalia have discovered things along the coastline or underwater while swimming with me that I never would have seen. Together with my wife Aspa they helped document all the swims with the videos and photos that accompany the book. Even more family members and friends have offered priceless bits of information that have all enriched my experiences on the island. I am also indebted to psychotherapist and surfer Greg Browne, marine biologist Dr. Stella Psarra, my uncle Manolis Drettakis, and million-yard swimmer David Miller for sharing their wisdom.

Since this is a guide for sightseeing from the water, I will not be providing substantial information about other aspects of touring Crete on land, such as accommodations. After you have trained to become a swimmer and after you have sought out information about touring the island, just like any other tourist, this book adds advice on swims that I personally enjoy and revisit every year. If you decide to stay on the western side of the island, then I have amazing swims for you there, and likewise if you choose the middle or eastern parts of Crete.

If you wish to try every swim, then you may need to stay two weeks or more. Even though the table of contents lists many locations for swimming, some places consist of multiple swims that can take multiple days. There are more than 50 swims in total that add up to over 100 km. Not only that, since there are at least 700 beaches on Crete and its satellite islands, your favorite swims may not be in my list. Yet, by bringing you to Crete with this book, an opportunity unfolds for you to create YOUR OWN unique marine travel journey.

1

Introduction

I HAVE NEVER BEEN A PROFESSIONAL ATHLETE. I'm just a guy who enjoys swimming—a *mere mortal* who goes slow on land and in water, eats too much, has not had a coach since playing water polo decades ago at the University of Michigan, feels pain when the water is cold, and doesn't seek any more medals or accolades. This book is written for mere mortals like me, yet more god-like swimmers will enjoy my swims as well.

Nevertheless, I am an experienced swimmer in pools and open water, particularly around the Greek island of [Crete](), birthplace of the *immortals* such as Zeus and the fifth largest island in the Mediterranean. I swim when the water is warm, approaching 27 °C (80 °F), and rarely swim for more than 90 minutes at a time. The same goes for lap swimming in a pool, where I typically spend 60 minutes swimming—again as a mere mortal—without a coach or a training schedule, and rarely more than three times a week.

Given my humble aquatic existence, why am I qualified to write a book on swimming? Well, this is really a book about swimming tourism in the amazing coastal waters surrounding Crete, located "in the midst of the wine-dark sea," as the ancient Greek poet Homer wrote nearly 3,000 years ago. I have spent three decades swimming all around the island and my swims are selected for the pleasure of exploring a new coastline and looking down at the seafloor through water that quite often offers visibility of 15 meters or more. My favorite swims have destinations that may be small islets, sea caves, Venetian fortresses, or the ruins of a civilization that thrived thousands of years ago. What you read in my book is the information I would give you if you happened to meet me somewhere on the island and asked for my top swimming recommendations, along with any safety concerns. Kayakers, snorkelers, and stand-up paddlers might also want to eavesdrop and venture out on my recommended routes.

There are times when I'm in the other person's shoes—I am the tourist, I have just arrived on a coastline that I've never seen before, it looks great for a swim, but I wish I had someone to ask for advice. Such as:

- Is it better to swim along the coast to the left, or to the right?
- Is there anything I should worry about?
- What about boats? Currents? Jellyfish?
- Are there any caves to explore?
- Is it worth circumnavigating that small island over there?
- If I come here at night, will I find bioluminescent plankton?
- And, by the way, can I park my car here?
- Where should I go for a drink and something to eat afterwards?

A wise ancient Greek philosopher named Thales of Miletus once asked, "What is the hardest thing to do?" The answer: "γνῶθι σεαυτόν" (GNO-thi se-af-TON) or *know thyself*. The next question was: "What is the easiest thing to do?" The answer: "Give others *advice*."

So, this is my disclaimer for the book: the advice I am providing is nothing more than my opinions about coastal water swims that I enjoy unsupervised on the island of Crete. I am not a health or sports professional, nor is my advice sanctioned by any organization in Greece or elsewhere. I am not your swim nanny.

If you know thyself, you will be able to figure out if the swims I am describing are something that you will enjoy, or something too dangerous for your level of swimming. When in doubt, ask an aquatics professional to evaluate your abilities. If all your swimming has been in a pool, then you should be extra cautious because you certainly do not know thyself in open water, yet.

Fortunately, for coastal water newbies, many of the swims in this book are less than a kilometer (km) round-trip, and the majority have possible courses within 25 meters (m) of the coastline—only Balos-Gramvousa places the swimmer more than 500 m from the coastline. And even the more dedicated rough-water swimmers will enjoy themselves—the island of Crete is a fantastic place for swimming and finding new adventures!

Orientation on Crete

Compared to the vast majority of the other 117 inhabited Greek islands, Crete is huge—you can't exactly see the entire place in just a few days. The drive from Falasarna beach on the west coast, to Vai beach on the east coast, is 337 km or roughly 5 hours without stops. By comparison, the famous island just north of Crete called Santorini can be traversed from north to south in about 45 minutes. The size of Crete therefore allows for a vast diversity of experiences, so much so that an insider like me can discover something new even after years of exploration. With a coastline totaling roughly 1,000 km, I may have sampled only a fifth of it so far. One could even refer to Crete as the "mainland" because it is surrounded by over 100 satellite islands.

Moreover, the culture of Crete is rather distinctive from the rest of Greece and one can gain great satisfaction as local art, music, food, history, and customs are revealed. Many visitors are astonished by the fresh ingredients used when dining in Crete, and at the very reasonable prices. Have you ever heard of the healthy Mediterranean diet? In Crete, this is simply called "eating." Also, Cretans have a well-deserved reputation for being generous and welcoming towards visitors. Did you know that after lunch or dinner in Crete it is customary for guests to be served a complimentary small dessert and the digestive called raki? (It's similar to Italian grappa.) Or, say that you ask the owner of a hotel what time you must check out. They might say something like, "It's at noon, but you can stay until two." I can't guarantee these things, but they tend to happen in Crete.

Crete has one main highway (E75) from west to east that passes through the four cities of Chania, Rethymno, Heraklion, and Agios Nikolaos on the north coast. Different roads branch southward from the main highway down to the south coast. It is possible to drive much of the south coast along a west-east route, but your progress will be slower. Thus, when you look at the 21 swim locations on the map below, it is a 75-minute drive between swims **#3** and **#8** on the north coast, but 155 minutes to travel between **#19** and **#14** along a southern route.

1. Balos-Gramvousa	6. The Green Coast	11. Mochlos & Richtis Waterfall	16. Agiofaraggo
2. Marathi Island	7. Paleokastro Caves	12. Vai Palm Beach	17. Matala's Hidden Sea Caves
3. Kamari Gastroswim	8. Knossos Final Approach	13. Xerokambos Falcon Islands	18. Agios Pavlos Full Moon Swim
4. Spilies Tunnel & Arch	9. Hersonnisos Coves	14. The Galactic Night Swim	19. The Amazing Gorge Swims
5. Bali (the one in Crete)	10. Artemisia's Swim	15. Treis Ekklisies Caves	20. Sfakia to Loutro to Marmara
			21. Elafonisi Eye Candy

Most tourists arrive in Crete by ferry boat or by air, landing mainly in Heraklion (airport code HER) or Chania (CHQ). Direct flights exist from many European cities—there is no need to fly through Athens (ATH) first.

High season begins in mid-July and lasts about six weeks. The absolute busiest 10 days begin August 15, which is a national holiday, and the Greeks customarily go on vacation to the villages, coastlines, and islands. Roads will be packed with cars, beaches crowded with people, and prices will be higher at hotels. The same holds true more generally for Sundays when businesses are closed, and everyone is heading to the beach. However, July and August are great months because the temperatures are warmest, and the days long. June and September are excellent alternatives because Crete is not quite as hot or crowded.

In September, the sea maintains its warmth from the hot summer months, but the days are noticeably shorter and there could be a few days of cloudy or rainy weather. In October you might say that the island 'returns to nature' when hotels and businesses start removing their umbrellas and chairs from the beaches. The roads become empty as well. If you desire abundant peace and quiet, even on the more populated northern coast, then you might like Crete best outside the June–September period.

Swimming for Sightseeing

Unlike other open water swimming books which might focus on training for speed and endurance, my goal is to help readers have a fantastic time sightseeing while swimming at a leisurely pace. This means they will be stopping often to appreciate the beauty of whatever lies below or around them, choosing destinations that might be a hidden cave, a secluded beach, or perhaps a short walk around archaeological ruins thousands of years old.

To enrich your adventure, you might try watching or reading two popular stories that take place on Crete. Nikos Kazantzakis, a highly regarded modern Greek author from Crete, published the novel *Zorba the Greek* in 1946. The 1964 black-and-white film adaptation starring Anthony Quinn won three Academy Awards. The final dance outdoors by the sea, which has the most recognizable Greek music in the universe ("Zorba's Dance" by Mikis Theodorakis), was filmed northwest of swim location **#2** at the village of Stavros. A more recent literary sensation is the book *The Island* by Victoria Hislop which was adapted as the 2010 hit television series "To Nisi" ("The Island"). It tells the story of one of Europe's last leper colonies on the island of Spinalonga which hosts a vast Venetian fortress. This is the location of swim **#10**.

Of course, Crete has been incredibly impactful in human history for many other reasons. The Minoan civilization flourished here five thousand years ago, and the epic Battle of Crete in 1941 was pivotal for countless people of the present day. As you travel to each of the swim locations, you will have many opportunities to enrich your soul by time-traveling to the past. And then, when you plunge into Crete's pristine waters, you might even be swimming in areas with coastal archaeological relics dating back thousands of years (particularly for locations **#6, 8, 11,** and **12**).

Many will be swimming to escape civilization and immerse themselves in Crete's marine ecosystem, made all the more staggering to behold by the extraordinary visibility of the water. Perhaps you will see a loggerhead sea turtle (*Caretta caretta*) gracefully meandering at a few meters depth. All beachgoers should keep an eye out for signage that indicates their nesting areas, and conservation groups such as Archelon can be contacted if an injured or dead turtle is found (rescue@archelon.gr).

Sharp-eyed swimmers might notice discrete piles of shells on the seafloor, a sure sign that an octopus is hiding just underneath. The occasional lionfish (*Pterois miles*) may be found lurking near rocks and dark areas posing for a photograph (see the photo below). They will not retreat from swimmers and should not be touched because of their venomous spines. In general, avoid touching or bumping into things. Even a small cone snail could be venomous, though a Triton's Trumpet (*Charonia tritonis*) can be handled gently. Stepping on sea urchins is a more obvious action to avoid, though I have failed every now and then—ouch!

Jellyfish are rare. Even rarer is the critically endangered Mediterranean monk seal (*Monachus monachus*), though one was seen recently at swim location **#6**. Topping that, friends reported sighting a sperm whale (*Physeter macrocephalus*) just 400 m off the coast at swim location **#20**. Cetaceans love Crete! That is because the Hellenic Trench—the Mediterranean Sea's deepest waters—starts northwest of Crete and arcs along the southern coastline. More can be learned about the marine ecosystem not just by swimming, but also by visiting the modern CretAquarium between swim locations **#8** and **#9**.

Swimmers should also consider how their activities may be a threat to the marine ecosystem. Though littering is an obvious action to avoid at all costs, it is also important to select sunscreens that minimize damage to the marine environment. It's a smart idea to avoid products that contain oxybenzone and octinoxate, and future scientific research may reveal other substances with a harmful impact.

Swimmers have a responsibility to educate themselves with respect to water safety when they plan swimming sightseeing. Safety can be improved if an escort vessel is present. A group of swimmers could try a do-it-yourself approach by renting kayaks or small motorized boats (e.g., at swim locations **#6** and **#20**).

For those with mobility challenges, some of the more developed beaches have cement and/or wood ramps over sand that lead from a parking area to within 5–20 m of the water. I believe that the beaches with the most accessible water entries are at swim locations **#2–4**, **6–8**, and **12** on the north coast, as well as swim locations **#14**, **18**, and **21** on the south coast. And, with over 700 beaches around the island, there are many other places to easily access the water that are not covered in this book. The only spot where I have seen a sunbed area designed for wheelchair access is Matala Beach (i.e., two sunbeds have extra height and rest on a wood deck constructed over the sand with a huge umbrella). One can check www.accessiblebeaches.gr for the latest updates on beach accessibility.

I think the blind and visually impaired may also enjoy these swims. Swimming from the open sea into a marine cave provides new sensations of changing temperature and sound. Navigating through the Spilies tunnel (**#4**) could be an interesting and rewarding task for a swimmer who would use echolocation to keep their heading on course. At Sweet Water Beach (**#20**), there are spots within 10 m of shore where cold, fresh water percolates upward from the seafloor, providing temperature and salinity landmarks for a course. Marine navigation is in fact one of the great challenges and rewards for anyone who attempts the coastal water swims in this book. The next section discusses this further.

Marine Navigation

Open water swimmers often reduce marine navigation to a single word: *sighting*. While swimming or floating, eyesight is used for navigation, swimming straight, and avoiding collisions.

The first ever mention of sighting is found in Homer's epic poem the [*Odyssey*](). After spending seven years imprisoned on an island by the goddess Calypso, the hero of the story—Odysseus—is allowed to leave on a raft, which is destroyed in a storm. As a mere mortal in the sea like me he needs to swim to survive:

> "Then for two nights and two days he was driven about over the swollen waves, and full often his heart forboded destruction. But when fair-tressed Dawn brought to its birth the third day, then the

wind ceased and there was a windless calm, and **he caught sight** of the shore close at hand, **casting a quick glance forward, as he was raised up by a great wave.**"

Ιδού (Behold): Homer taught sighting 2,800 years ago! When the crest of a wave lifts a swimmer, that is the best time to look forward in order to catch sight of a landmark.

However, sighting is just one aspect of marine navigation and a better term to use is *piloting*. Understanding where you are (your position *fix*) and where you are heading depends on much more than just sight. Experienced swimmers will perceive their direction and location using the warmth of the sun, the feeling of the oncoming wind and waves, sound (as he swam, Odysseus could hear breaking waves that told him the direction of reefs before he could actually see them), odors, proprioception (innate knowledge of one's body position and motion), the sense of time, and *path integration* (*dead reckoning*).

Path integration refers to keeping track of self-motion. If you can remember a sequence of decisions to go straight, turn right or left, and how far you went in space and time for each leg, then that sum of vectors defines a path which shows where you are now relative to your starting point. Thus, when a dense fog prevents mariners from piloting using visual landmarks, they must rely on path integration instead. This might seem completely unreliable, but I will never forget as a kid crewing a sailboat for my friend Chris Tuckfield in a race that suffered from white-out fog. I had no idea where we were on the water, but Chris navigated with astonishing precision back to the finish line with no GPS information. That was an example of path integration at its finest.

WARNING: All the other sailboats in that race got lost and did not manage to find the finish line! Marine path integration is difficult, but can be improved through training, practice, and experience. Chris and I would spend hours in his back yard walking around with model sailboats in our hands, studying what happens with different bearings relative to the wind. Open water swimmers can improve their marine navigation skills as well while they walk on land, keeping track of their motion relative to the cardinal directions, landmarks, and the wind. For example, you can ask yourself what direction is the wind coming from, how strong is it, and if you were in the water, which direction would you sight forward to compensate for the wind and stay on course?

Most of the time we are navigating using sighting and path integration simultaneously. A relationship between you and a landmark is called an *egocentric* or *me*-centered representation ("I am swimming 25 m from shore") whereas a relationship between landmarks is called an *allocentric* or *other*-centered representation ("the island is 650 m southeast of the beach"). The maps provided in this book will give you allocentric information that should be reviewed before you enter the water for the egocentric experience which will involve sighting.

All the maps in this book have an orientation with *true north* (the direction of Earth's north pole) pointing up. *Magnetic north* (magnetic declination) is roughly 5° east for Crete, which is relatively insignificant for our purposes, but could interest swimmers who practice precision navigation using compasses.

For those swimmers interested in the history of navigation technology, consider the Minoan ruins on the island of Mochlos (location **#11** on the map). A geoscientist named W.S. Downey finds that the orientations of buildings (strike directions) appear to align with the magnetic north direction of 4,000 years ago instead of true north. (The direction of magnetic north changes over time and 4,000 years ago it pointed 18° east of true north.) Thus, it stands to reason that Minoan marine navigation used compasses some 4,000 years ago. If this theory is proven true, it contradicts the current belief that the Chinese invented the magnetic compass around 200 BCE. In actuality, it could be a much older tool.

Allow me to offer a quick orientation regarding the cardinal directions, better known as the four points of the compass (going clockwise): north, east, south, and west. East is the direction where the sun rises in the morning and west is the direction where it sets in the evening. Between sunrise and sunset, and particularly at mid-day, the sun is in the southern sky (assuming a Northern Hemisphere location such as Greece). If the wind is a "westerly," that means it is blowing *from* the west to the east. In other words, a wind that will push a swimmer *eastward* is a *westerly* wind. A northwesterly wind would be one blowing *from* a direction that is in between west and north. If a beach is "facing" southeast, that means that as you swim straight out from the beach, you are swimming to the southeast. If you veer to the left, you are turning eastward. If you veer to the right, you are turning southward. If you make a U-turn and head back to the beach, you are swimming to the northwest. If you have a northwesterly wind, the wind will be blowing against you as you swim back to the beach.

Next, I am going to define seven more navigation terms (in bold) that I adapted from my experiences in both nautical and aeronautical piloting. My goal is to simplify the terminology, providing for the basic needs of a swimmer.

The swimmer's head is like the bow of a vessel and the direction that the body is pointing is called the ***heading*** (in sailing this is called the "course steered"). The ground ***track*** is the body's motion relative to fixed landmarks and the sea bottom from a bird's eye view. In still water with no wind, the swimmer's heading traces their track. However, the body can be pushed by both a water current and the wind. By adding these two types of pushes together we obtain a ***drift*** vector. A vector is an arrow that encodes a speed (e.g., 6 km/h) and direction or angle (e.g., southeast). To estimate drift, a swimmer can stop, float, and watch the coastline, the seafloor, or an anchored object such as a boat or buoy. A GPS device can also help.

Notice that the push due to wind is applied directly against the swimmer's body, an effect called ***leeway*** in sailing. When you see a beach umbrella tumbling across a beach because of the wind, that is leeway. If you get in a car and drive 35 km/h with your hand out the window on a still day, you will be able to simulate the leeway due to a 5 Beaufort wind (described later in this chapter). When swimming directly against a high wind I might change to breaststroke to keep most of my body underwater and minimize leeway. Swimming with a strong wind to your back is fun because leeway turbocharges a swimmer's forward motion.

When the drift angle is in the same or opposite direction as the heading, the ground track speed will be faster or slower, respectively. What happens if the drift vector is NOT parallel to the heading? The ground track will deviate by some angle relative to the heading.

Angles increase clockwise and are 0° for north, 90° for east, 180° for south, and 270° for west. Angles can be easier to understand by using the terminology of a clock, where 0° is 12 o'clock, 90° is 3 o'clock, and so forth. Thus, if someone says "check your 6" that means look directly behind you at 6 o'clock. Yet another synonym for angle is the word ***bearing***. For example, one can say that a straight-line track from west to east has a 90° *bearing* relative to true north.

CRETE SWIM

Finally, I define the word *course* (or route) as designating the path that you intend to follow relative to fixed landmarks or points. A *course* is a hypothetical path, whereas a ground *track* is a record of actual positions over time. If I anchor three buoys in the water, then that defines a course in the shape of a triangle. If you are doing a great job piloting, your track follows your course—they are basically the same thing. If you have not adjusted your heading to compensate for drift, then your track will be *off course*. Finally, the distance to a destination is referred to as the *range*.

As an example, let's look at Artemisia's Swim from the island of Spinalonga returning to the starting beach. You are *sighting* to swim a straight-line *course* to the beach northwest of Spinalonga with *range* 1 km. However, a wind is blowing perpendicular to your body from the right (from the northeast), and this creates a water current and *leeway* which defines your *drift vector* towards the southwest. If you choose a *heading* that is a straight line to the beach, the *drift* will push your *track* from a bird's eye view to the west and you will go *off course*. Therefore, you should change your *heading* to a relative *bearing* 45° away from the *course* direction and *into* the wind. The combination of your swimming propulsion forward and drift to your left will create a track that is *on course* to the beach. When you sight directly forward you will NOT see the beach destination. Instead, you will sight a relative *bearing* that is 45° to the right of the beach.

Some open water swimming literature mistakenly states that if someone wishes to swim a straight-line course to a destination, they should sight forward, and their track will stay on course. However, if the drift vector is not oriented exactly along the intended route, the swimmer will stay on course only if they sight an angle away from the destination, into the current or wind. Sighting forward is NOT the direction of the swimmer's track or course in this situation.

Even though the range is 1 km in this example, notice that this is NOT a 1-km swim in terms of time and effort. Your swimming vector is oriented 45° to the right (clockwise) of your course (destination). This means that your progress in the direction towards the destination is diminished by some factor, which in this case is cosine (45°) = 0.71. Therefore, your speed towards the beach is 1.4 times slower (1 / 0.71) than your swimming speed. Suppose you already know that in open water you can swim 1 km in 30 minutes when there is no current or wind to cause drift. In this example, the 1-km swim will take approximately 42 minutes

(1.4 x 30 minutes). For reference, if your relative bearing is 20°, 40°, or 60°, then you are slower on the course by a factor of 1.1, 1.3, and 2.0, respectively.

Determining what angle to use for your heading and estimating the total swim time is an iterative process—you will be changing your bearing as you figure out what seems to work best each time you assess your progress. The sea is a dynamic environment.

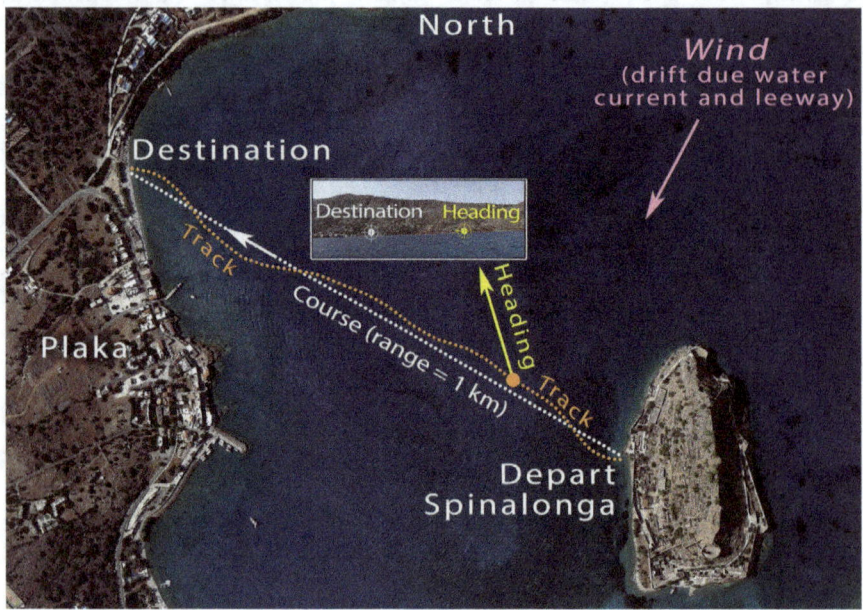

It is also worth considering that *the fastest course may not be a straight line* to the destination. In the excursion shown above, you could allow the drift to push you due west, and once you are within 30 m of shore, where you have anticipated that the drift might be negligible, swim northward to your destination. Thus, the *course* has two segments at different *bearings* to reach your destination. This seems like a greater distance of swimming, but it may take less time and effort. The problem in this particular case is the presence of boat traffic if the swimmer chooses a course due west.

Swimmers and anyone else piloting on the water always have strategic choices to make. The figure below illustrates a common situation where a swimmer wishes to cross a bay. The shortest distance from the starting point to the destination is a straight line 275 m into the wind against rough seas. Hugging the coastline in calm water *protected* from the wind is a longer distance of 325 m. Yet, if the rough seas reduce the swim speed by 50%, the straight-line course equates to a 550 m effort. Hugging the coastline is therefore a wiser choice. By the same token, it makes sense to return to the starting point by crossing the bay in a straight line because the weather will make the pace 50% faster. Thus, the swimmer's course could be a counterclockwise loop as shown in the figure.

How does a swimmer know that the weather will have a 50% effect on their pace? Essentially, they need to try such swims to gain experience. In this particular example, they could depart the starting point and swim 50 m into the straight-line crossing, stop, float, assess how fast the wind and current are pushing them backwards, and then decide if they should continue in a straight line across the bay or hug the coast.

Sighting Tips: What should you be looking at and how often? The answers depend on your *goals*, *relative swim speed*, and *conditions*. I just mentioned that we sight forward to pinpoint our destination and heading, as well as to swim straight along our heading. I recommend spending at least one second looking forward, which is the time it takes to mentally say the words, "Say cheese," as if posing for a photograph. We also sight forward so that we do not collide with another swimmer coming the other way, or to follow another swimmer. In wavy water, it makes sense to time a sighting when at the top (*crest*) of a wave, just as Homer wrote in the *Odyssey*. Even so, another swimmer may be at the bottom (*trough*) of a wave at that exact time, and you will not see them. The same goes for debris or marine life. Thus, we need to sight often to better know what lies ahead.

Let's work through one example where your swim route is fairly routine, and your main *goal* is to avoid colliding with other open water swimmers. You probably know your pace, such as 100 m in two minutes. If other swimmers have the same pace, but they are coming from the other direction, then your *relative swim speed* is 100 m in one minute. It's equivalent to magically swimming twice as fast towards a stationary object. If the *conditions* are such that you can only spot a swimmer 50 m in front of you, then you are 30 seconds away from a collision. Therefore, you should aim to sight forward every 15 seconds (or less) to avoid colliding. In practice, you also need to measure your stroke rate. I found that in 15 seconds my right hand enters the water nine times, which tells me to sight forward every ninth stroke cycle in this example.

Sighting forward we are also checking for breaking waves (surf) that indicate shallow areas. Likewise, we are sighting to either side, scanning for other swimmers, boats, buoys, landmarks, and our position relative to the sun (or, in the case of night swims, artificial lights, the moon, and stars). Finally, given excellent underwater visibility, we are also looking down for underwater landmarks.

One could argue that sighting actually begins on the beach where we cannot allow ourselves to be in a hurry. Instead, for safety's sake, one should slow down and become mindful of the environment. The wind direction, its strength, and the possibility of gusts need to be studied. Sighting nearby and distant flags is usually the best option, but in their absence, we can pick up some sand and let it fall to the ground to determine the wind direction. Check the direction that anchored boats are pointing to estimate the local currents and winds in the water (boats with a single anchor are like wind vanes). In case there are breaking waves and surfers, check how the surfers paddle out to sea because they might be using a rip current. If there is a marina or boat-rental facility, note the buoys that define the lane for incoming and outgoing boat traffic. Look to greater distances and sight the larger buoys that may be used by jet skiers. Scan the entire sea for larger boats that may be approaching, departing, or taking a course near the coastline. Finally, look at everything else around and behind the beach and ask yourself, "If I am 500 m out at sea, how would I recognize this beach and what makes it unique relative to the beaches on either side?" After entering the water, pause after 50 m of swimming and look back to the beach and review the landmarks again.

Finally, sighting a *transit line* is a useful navigation technique for identifying your location in relation to a line defined by two fixed landmarks, helping you establish and maintain a course. For example, while swimming away from a beach, you can sight *backwards* and observe that your track aligns precisely with a line formed by a distant mountain peak and a building in the foreground. When you return to this area an hour later, sighting along this same transit line will guide you straight to the beach. The landmarks for a transit line could also be situated to your left and right or forward and backward. If two transit lines are available at the same time, their intersection gives a fix on your location (as in 'x marks the spot'). The next section illustrates how sighting transit lines can be very helpful.

Understand Sighting Illusions: Knowing your position fix in the sea without consulting a GPS device requires your senses, particularly your eyesight, and thus we are all susceptible to position and distance illusions. A classic illusion is that the perception of size, brightness, and distance are interdependent, creating errors in accurately judging them. If you have ever seen the moon appear huge as it rises over the horizon, then that is one of those illusions where you perceive an incorrect angular size because you innately assume an incorrect distance. Indeed, open water swimming exposes the senses to vast expanses of space and size scales that are completely different from a cityscape or areas inside a home. For example, if you wish to cross a bay where you see a large mountain at the other end, you may judge that range as smaller than it really is because you think that something large is closer to you. The solution is to be aware of these illusions, question your senses, seek other lines of evidence to gauge a distance, and then learn from the experience. For example, try standing on a beach and noting how large a person standing on a different beach appears to be. Then using a map, check the range between the two beaches (e.g., 400 m), and try to remember how large a standing person looks like at that distance.

The **Heading Rotation Error (HRE)** occurs when we believe we are swimming straight towards a destination, but from a bird's eye view our heading is rotating around it. This occurs when the destination appears small in front of us (i.e., small in size or a great distance away), other fixed reference points are absent, and we cannot perceive that we are being moved sideways by the wind and current.

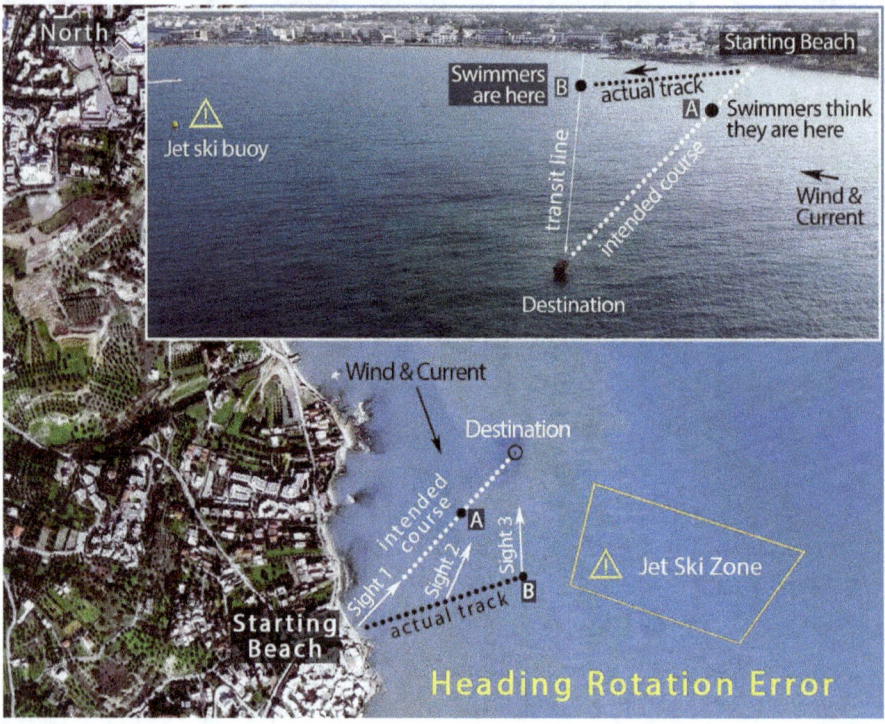

The example figure shows an intended course from the starting beach to a small rock in the sea (swim **#9**, Hersonissos Coves). There are no other reference points between the swimmer and the rock, nor past the rock to the horizon. If all we have in a scene is a distant rock and the horizon, one could rotate 360° around the rock and not perceive any changes whatsoever in our visual field.

Three short arrows indicate the direction that the swimmer is sighting forward, i.e., the swimmer's body points in the direction of each arrow and defines their heading. Each time they sight forward the swimmer has the illusion that they are located exactly on their intended course swimming towards their destination. In reality, the wind and current have pushed them off course and their actual track points towards a dangerous jet ski zone. Over time, the swimmer's heading *rotated* from the initial northeasterly direction to due north. Because the landmarks are small or at great distances in front of them, both the 45° rotation and their off-course position will go unnoticed. The swimmer thinks they are at position *A* when in fact they are at position *B*. The small destination and the horizon look exactly the same in front of them from both *A* and *B*.

The solution is for the swimmer to occasionally *sight backwards* and check if they are on a transit line between their starting beach and destination. At "Sight 2" they would notice that the starting beach is no longer in the opposite direction of their destination. At "Sight 3" they would find that the starting beach is to the left of their heading and exactly behind them are landmarks due south. If it's a sunny day, they might also notice their heading relative to the sun has changed. To get back on course, the swimmer would have to change their heading so that it points into the wind and current. If they cannot return to their intended course and stay on course, they would need to call the swim and head back to shore.

The **Projected Shape Error** (PSE) accounts for how we judge the shape and size of a distant landmark such as an island based on its one-dimensional or two-dimensional appearance in front of us. Imagine holding a pencil in your hand and shining a light on it in a dark room. The shadow on the wall is the projected shape, and you can rotate the pencil to make this shape smaller than the true size of the pencil. So too, an island could have any shape as seen from a bird's eye view, but the swimmer sees only one side. That side has an apparent total length from left to right—let's say 100 m—and in our minds we might use this information to classify the island as "small" or "large." If we then assume that an island has four equal sides, circumnavigating the island is simply four times the length of the side we are viewing—400 m in this example. However, if the island is shaped like a pencil, where we have approached the island from the pointy end, and its true depth towards the horizon is 1 km, then we would have over 2 km of swimming to circumnavigate the island. We may be making the same mistake many times over as we swim along coastlines where we judge the depth of what we see to be smaller than it really is. In the same example, once we arrive at the pencil-shaped island and start swimming along its long coastline, we will understand it has a long shape, but we still may not be aware of how far we really must go to reach the far end of the pencil.

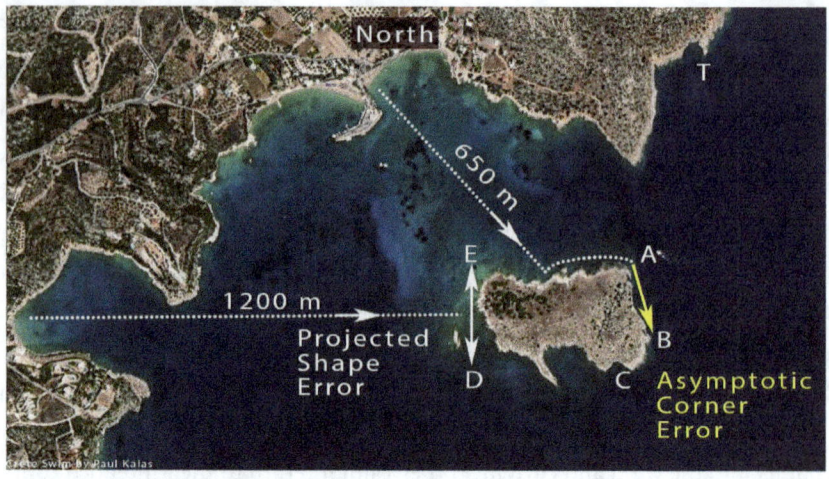

Another particularly tricky and common sighting illusion concerns finding your position relative to a curved landmark. The swimmer will believe they are sighting the corner of an island or cape, but in actuality their line of sight is an asymptote to a curve. The true corner is farther away along the curved surface, out of sight. I call this the **Asymptotic Corner Error** or **ACE**. I'll bet that the ancient Greek mathematicians such as Euclid discovered the principles of geometry simply because a vibrant sea-faring civilization needed mathematical rules for navigation. Geometry and measurements of time were created for the mariners.

However, don't panic if a navigation error occurs in your swim. A healthy sense of humor always helps. When you discover that the corner you just struggled to swim to is just halfway to the real destination, turn to your swim buddy with a smile and say, "Ha, we've been ACE'd!" Try to learn from these mistakes and become a better Greek navigator.

Swim location **#2**, Marathi Island (see Chapter 3), illustrates both PSE and ACE. Swimmers can approach either the west or north coast of the island. Choosing the 650-m route from the northwest, swimmers arrive in the middle of the north coast and then head east to circumnavigate the island clockwise. When arriving at the first corner (**A**), one sights forward (to the south) and believes that point **B** is the southeast corner of the island. However, this is an example of ACE because point **C** is the real southeast corner of the island, 85 m away from **B**. One way for a swimmer to know when they have arrived at **B** vs. **C** is to sight a transit line northward toward **T**. If the swimmer can still see **T**, then they have not yet arrived at **C**.

The 1.2-km approach from the west illustrates PSE. Swimmers will see that the width of the island between **D** and **E** is roughly 250 m. The assumption would be that circumnavigating the island is a 1-km swim. However, the depth of the island in the east–west direction is 450 m, and the circumnavigation distance is closer to 1.4 km.

Though these navigation errors may seem easily overcome by swimming a bit farther, the reader should not underestimate the psychological impact. Having to swim farther and spend more time in the water than expected can create a feeling of dread that one is lost. Moreover, the extra 85 m between points **B** and **C** is a stretch where swimmers lose sight of the mainland, the sea is deeper and darker, and the area becomes more exposed to rough water.

Even Odysseus experienced a great foreboding when swimming towards land and his hopes for survival turned to dread when he could not find a safe water exit:

> "But when he was as far away as a man's voice carries when he shouts, and heard the boom of the sea upon the reefs—for the great wave thundered against the dry land, belching upon it in terrible fashion, and all things were wrapped in the foam of the sea; for there were neither harbors where ships might ride, nor road-steads, but projecting headlands, and reefs, and cliffs—then the knees of Odysseus were loosened and his heart melted, and deeply moved he spoke to his own mighty spirit:

> 'Ah me, when Zeus has at length granted me to see the land beyond my hopes, and lo, I have prevailed to cleave my way and to cross this gulf, nowhere doth there appear a way to come forth from the grey sea. For without are sharp crags, and around them the wave roars foaming, and the rock runs up sheer, and the water is deep close in shore, so that in no wise is it possible to plant both feet firmly and escape ruin. Haply were I to seek to land, a great wave may seize me and dash me against the jagged rock, and so shall my striving be in vain. But if I swim on yet further in hope to find shelving beaches and harbors of the sea, I fear

me lest the storm-wind may catch me up again, and bear me, groaning heavily, over the teeming deep; or lest some god may even send forth upon me some great monster from out the sea—and many such does glorious Amphitrite breed.'"

This passage is wonderful and deadly serious because it spells out the debate of an open water swimmer confronted with choices that need to be made within the context of unexpected and disheartening events. It was hard for Odysseus to know if continuing the swim along the coast would be a fatal mistake. He decided to take this risk and eventually found a safe beach at the mouth of a river.

Hopefully this section has provided some insights on how to avoid navigation mistakes. Nonetheless, mistakes are expected to happen—our eyes can fool us—and it is best to stay calm and be confident in our skills when we are surprised or experience fear.

Weather Conditions (June–September)

The **water temperature** is coldest in early June (21 °C or 70 °F) and approaches 27 °C (80 °F) in July, August, and September as the Mediterranean warms up with the summer sunshine. These are rough guidelines because shallow water will be warmer, deeper water colder, coastal areas with percolating mountain springs the coldest, and of course the sun and wind have their obvious roles in heating and cooling the surface layers of the sea as well as your body. For comparison, regulations for a competition pool in the United States specify a water temperature between 25.6° and 26.7 °C (78–80 °F). Therefore, the water around Crete may feel slightly colder than a swimming pool. Also, before entering the water, the sun will be warming your body so that submerging suddenly, even in the summer when the water is warmest, may still give you a "cold shock" that can cause a medical emergency. These factors will be discussed further when safety issues are reviewed.

Visibility in the water is typically very good at over 15 meters. I have refrained from mentioning visibility for each swim because turbulent conditions can make the water murkier. Moreover, each swim might transition from murkier water in some parts (e.g., sandy, shallow areas) to amazing clarity in others (e.g., rocky, deeper water), and this may change during the course of a day.

Rainy days will be rare, but not entirely impossible, within the four-month period between June and September. I would recommend refraining from swimming for a few days after significant rain because the coastal waters could be polluted with storm runoff.

Otherwise, expect strong sunshine and protect your skin according to your individual needs. You may need to wear a "rash guard" or "swim shirt" to protect your upper body from the sun, particularly for mid-day swims.

Tidal Streams and Rip Currents: Open water swimmers (and kayakers as well) should always contemplate how astronomical *tides* will impact their swim. Tides are the changes of water level between lows and highs each day due to gravity between the Sun, Earth, and Moon. Increasing the vertical height of water is called *flooding* and decreasing it is called *ebbing*. Flooding and ebbing create a type of horizontal water current called a *tidal stream*.

For Crete, the minimum to maximum variation of the tide is roughly 30 cm (12 in), and the precise times of the daily highs and lows are found online in tide charts or tables. In my opinion, it is not necessary to worry about tides for the swims in this book. **Strong currents will be due to wind rather than tidal streams.** Nevertheless, consider the following:

- If during high tide you swam over a very shallow rocky area, say with just 30 cm of clearance between your chest and rock, that same area may be impassable when you return during low tide.
- If during high tide you swam safely over a somewhat shallow area, say with 100 cm of clearance between your chest and rock, and there were gentle waves, that same area may be dangerous with stronger breaking waves during low tide.
- Passing through tunnels and exploring caves may have different safety margins depending on the tidal water level and currents.
- Note that a night swim may take place many hours after one has checked an area for safety during the day and one should contemplate what aspects of the swim will be different if the water level is different.

- Water level height can also increase due to storm surges, and this may be more important for swimming around Crete than the astronomical tide. The "storm" is not necessarily a hurricane, but characterized by strong winds under clear, summertime skies farther out to sea. In Greek this is often referred to as a "φουσκωμένη θάλασσα" (foo-sko-MENI THA-la-sa) or an "inflated sea."

In addition to the currents caused by astronomical tides and wind, swimmers should always study beaches with breaking waves to understand the location of a *rip current*. The large mass of water that hits a beach must return to sea, and these currents tend to occur in channels perpendicular to the shoreline. If you enter the water in a part of the beach where there is a rip current, you will more easily be taken out to sea. Some people may do this on purpose as a strategic decision to aid in their swim. Others may enter the rip current by accident and find that they cannot swim back to shore.

This is a dangerous situation because swimming against the current is exhausting and can lead to drowning. The key is to quickly **Recognize (R)** that you are in a rip current, **Accept (A)** that you have a problem that cannot be solved by brute force, and then **Swim Parallel (SP) to shore** until you exit the channel current. Only *then* would you turn to swim towards shore. Quite often, swimming 100 m parallel to shore (2–3 minutes of relaxed swimming) will be enough. Then make that 90° turn towards shore.

I would try to memorize a short mnemonic such as **RASP** because we do not do our best thinking when emergencies strike. One needs to train and practice good habits in order to react quickly and correctly when rare but dangerous events become a reality. From personal experience I think that *A* is a critical juncture: we often cannot accept that a current is too strong and deplete our strength fighting it. This speaks to that difficult problem of knowing ourselves. *SP*, on the other hand, is an excellent example of the navigation lessons from the previous section—our heading (sighting forward) *does not* point to our destination. Instead, we are going to swim *perpendicular* to our beach destination for 2–3 minutes, which seems highly counterintuitive as if making a grave mistake. Yet, this is the correct navigation decision to exit a rip current and return to shore.

Wind: The most common winds between June and September are the northerlies or northwesterlies. During July and August, much of Greece experiences the "meltemi" (mel-TEH-me) wind which is generally a northerly at five or more Beaufort (>30 km/h). It builds during the day and might continue all night. The weather will appear clear, and the winds may continue for many consecutive days. The exact wind direction at each location along the Cretan coastline will vary as the wind coming from the north over the open water encounters and wraps around the mountains and their associated thermal effects. Beaches along the north coast of Crete will have larger waves with an onshore wind and conversely, the south coast will have offshore winds. Both coasts have many bays and peninsulas that protect swimmers from the northwesterly weather, and my goal here is to explain these important details.

The sea currents for the swims are mainly driven by the strong winds. Before any swim, find out which way the wind is blowing. The sea current will most likely be in this direction too, or slightly to the right of it. Given a wind that has been blowing for a few hours, the current might be 0.02 times the wind speed. It may not sound like much, but a very common summer breeze of 20 km/h equates to a sea current of 400 m per hour. So, if you were expecting to reach a destination 2 km away in one hour, you may end up 400 m short at the end of an hour if you were swimming against this current. Given a person who is at their limit with respect to dehydration, hypothermia, or fatigue after one hour of swimming, falling 400 m short would be dangerous for them.

It is essential to monitor the daily wind reports, observe rapidly changing wind conditions locally, and check the wind forecasts. Wind reports and forecasts are available through various apps and websites such as www.windfinder.com. Be careful to note when a page is showing a model prediction versus a real recent measurement. One must also watch out for broken weather stations by double-checking the time and date stamp of a weather update.

One of the more reliable stations is for Heraklion airport: www.windfinder.com/report/heraklion_airport

A graphical, interactive map of beach conditions is available here: www.meteo.gr/beaches-home.cfm

After years of open water swimming and other marine activities, I am accustomed to gauging wind in terms of the Beaufort wind force scale and knots.

One knot is 1.852 km/h. For comparison, a typical walking speed is 5 km/h. Note that the weather forecast displayed on Greek television will usually show the Beaufort scale. So, if you see a map of Greece marked with an arrow pointing down labeled 4–5, that means northerly winds at 4–5 Beaufort. The table summarizes what the Beaufort scale translates to.

Beaufort	knots	km/h	Appearance
0	<1	<1	Completely calm; a glassy sea surface.
1	1–3	1–5	Puffs of wind.
2	4–6	6–11	Light breeze.
3	7–10	12–19	Gentle breeze, few whitecaps.
4	11–16	20–28	Breezy, choppy, scattered whitecaps.
5	17–21	29–38	Windy, whitecaps with some spray.
6	22–27	39–49	Strong wind, whitecaps everywhere, spray.

The scale continues upwards to 12 (hurricane). In my opinion, if I see a weather forecast for 1–3 Beaufort, I consider that a "light" wind day. At four Beaufort, I would expect a choppy open sea and be cautious that it could increase to five Beaufort during the day. Within the five Beaufort range, I would expect the lower end of 17 knots to feel windy with a choppy sea, but for the high end of 21 knots, I would expect a strong wind that lifts the sand off the beach and hits me painfully. At 5–6 Beaufort, I would seek protected areas to swim, stay close to shore, check for currents, double-check for currents, and generally limit my swim.

Exactly what you will encounter as a swimmer depends on the wind direction, topography, and other factors. Personally, I feel comfortable swimming within 50 m of a beach in a six Beaufort wind when I am on the south coast of Crete and it is blowing offshore or side shore. The water will be flat with intense, stinging spray, and I will pay extra attention to the current by stopping frequently to see how I am drifting. Conversely, it could be a beautiful 3–4 Beaufort day on Crete, but I may NOT enter the water on the north coast because significant waves are coming southward from more intense northerly winds hitting the open sea north of the island. In other words, the Beaufort scale may underestimate wave conditions because strong waves can be generated far from the island.

Let's take a look at a real-life example of comparing actual conditions versus wind measurements. One day in September I arrived at Mades (mah-DES) Beach on the Green Coast (location **#6**), which faces north, and I felt a steady onshore breeze, with occasional gusts that I would call "windy" as opposed to "breezy." The water looked a little choppy 100 m in front of me and, 500 m away towards the open sea, I saw hints of white caps. I also saw the white splash of waves crashing on a rocky point one kilometer to the right. I entered the water, and the chop was worse than it looked from shore. I had to be very careful not to swallow water as I swam against the weather. I had to maintain a strong kick and stopped frequently to assess the current. Staring at the sea bottom for a few seconds, I perceived that I was being pushed downwind (though not faster than I could swim). I thought to myself that the swim would have been difficult for my kids if they had been with me. I continued my swim 50 m at a time in order to rest and double-check conditions.

Exactly how windy was it that day? My portable anemometer showed that what I would call an onshore "breeze" on the beach was only 5 knots (9 km/h) and the strongest wind gusts were 9 knots (17 km/h). In other words, measurements showed this was a 2–3 Beaufort day, which should have been an easy swim. Yet, by choosing a north-facing beach, the sea had the increased difficulty and risk of a 4–5 Beaufort day because the entire swim was exposed to the northerlies that produced tougher wave conditions. If I had tried the swim at the Peninsula Hotel nearby, which faces south, I probably would have concluded that it was indeed an "easy swim" day.

The moral of the story is to never dive in the water and continue a swim based on what you previously saw, knew, or expected. **Avoid wishful thinking.** Your swimming conditions are not what they are "supposed to be"—they are nothing more or less than what is actually happening when you are in the water.

PERSONAL JOURNAL
Date | Time | Swim

2

The Basics: Safety, Gear & Preparation

DROWNING IS THE SECOND HIGHEST CAUSE OF DEATH after road accidents in Greece during the summer, according to an article published in *The National Herald* (July 29, 2019). Writing a travel adventure book focused on swimming has a Catch–22: providing opinions on coastal water swims is intended to *help* with safety, yet no matter what one says or does, swimming is potentially *deadly*. The article continues with the following:

> "The Hellenic Institute for Occupational Health and Safety said the biggest problem is that most people think they are better swimmers and aren't able to confront a problem in the water when it happens. Greece's drowning death numbers per capita is among the world's highest. The group advised never to swim alone, not to swim if they are in a bad physical or mental state, to wait three hours after a heavy meal, and never to swim under the influence of alcohol or drugs."

I discuss safety topics in every chapter and the next section will focus on it, followed by two more topics that are related to safety: swimming gear and preparation. First and foremost, note that the following phone numbers can be dialed to report an emergency:

112 is the free number to dial or text for all types of emergencies, 24/7, in Greece or anywhere in the European Union.

108 is the free number to reach the Coast Guard directly, but 112 will also connect you to that agency or any other emergency service that may be needed.

In my opinion, unsupervised (without local guides or support vessels) coastal water swims can be as dangerous as flying a plane solo. You can train for several months and then fly a plane solo successfully your entire life, but mistakes, accidents, and Mother Nature can be deadly. The safety nets are few. For an unsupervised coastal water swim, you need to be in the same mindset as a pilot flying solo. For each flight, the pilot studies the weather conditions and forecasts, prepares and checks equipment, achieves and maintains a certain skill level, is physically and mentally healthy, creates a flight plan that is communicated to others, and is willing and able to make calm, on-the-fly decisions for the sake of safety as conditions change. The same goes for coastal water swimming. And just like flying a plane, the reward will be the thrill of traveling through new environments with amazing views, and the satisfaction of mastering new challenges on your own.

Safety Tips

My recommended swim courses and safety tips are based on personal experiences swimming around Crete from June through September in 1–4 Beaufort conditions and they may not be adequate for other months or circumstances that are rare (a thunderstorm in the middle of July, for example). Therefore, I will not be covering cold-water safety guidelines for winter swims.

Advice about safety is also provided by swimming-related groups worldwide and likely exists in your native language. For example, the Honolulu City and County Lifeguards have the following safety tips:

- Swim in Lifeguarded Areas
- Never Swim Alone
- Don't Dive Into Unknown Water or Into Shallow Breaking Waves
- Ask a Lifeguard About Beach and Surf Conditions Before Swimming
- If You Are Unable to Swim Out of a Strong Current, Signal for Help

- Rely on Your Swimming Ability Rather Than a Flotation Device
- Look For, Read and Obey All Beach Safety Signs and Symbols

Regarding the final point about safety signs:

- A green flag at a beach in Greece and elsewhere usually means "swim freely."
- A yellow flag denotes "swim at your own risk."
- A red flag warns "dangerous conditions, do not enter the water."
- An orange windsock indicates strong offshore winds and that inflatable objects should not be used in the water.

In practice however, the majority of beaches in Crete do not have lifeguards or beach safety signs. Moreover, lifeguards work certain hours, and you may wish to swim before they arrive or after they depart. Indeed, given the strong sun during the summer in Crete, there are incentives to swim early in the morning or later in the afternoon. Lifeguards may go home around 5 pm, yet during the summer months, one can swim several hours after that in daylight.

Also, note that sea buoys are used in organized open water swims to mark a course, but in our case, most sea buoys are meant for watercraft and the swimmer should stay away from them. For example, two parallel strings of small red buoys are often placed to mark a marine traffic *lane* perpendicular to the beach for rental craft use. If a swimmer needs to cross this lane, they should do it quickly after waiting for the lane to clear of any departing or approaching watercraft. If possible, enter and exit the water at a point on the beach where you would NOT have to cross the lane as a swimmer.

A second example is one or more large yellow buoys in deeper water. These are positioned to define a boundary within which recreational craft such as jet skis are asked to remain. If you see one large yellow buoy, a second one probably exists farther away, and jet skis would be expected to travel back and forth between them. A swimmer should pause on the beach or in the water to search for these buoys and understand how they may define dangerous areas for swimmers. **Do not swim near the large buoys** since jet skiers may circle them.

The powered watercraft you will typically see are jet skis, boats of various sizes for 10–100 people operated by licensed tour operators, fishing boats, recreational vessels used by local Greeks, and small 4–10 person rental boats. The peak marine traffic days are fine-weather Sunday's when the local Cretans are out on the water in addition to the daily tourism-related vessels. Regardless of the day of the week, these watercrafts are all a threat to swimmers and the figures in this book show **a triangle warning sign for areas likely to have boats.** On the other hand, each boat is a potential safety resource for the swimmer to request a rescue.

In fact, the availability of powered rental boats offers the possibility for swimmers themselves to rent them as escort vessels. The swims in this book do not assume the availability of a boat—for the most part you will be hugging the coastlines and using beaches accessible by roads. With an escort boat, swimmers could be more ambitious with their distances and courses. Or one can use the boat to reach isolated destinations. That way swimmers can explore more remote areas without having to swim all that way to see them. So, if there is anyone among your family and friends who is licensed to pilot a boat, make sure they remember to bring their license to Crete.

Note that some rental boat operators do not even require a license, but this can be very risky. I recall rescuing a party of four Italians in a small rental boat who tried to cross from Sardinia to Corsica and became stuck in the middle when their engine failed. They flagged down our sailboat and fortunately someone in our party knew how to restart their motor. There was nothing wrong with it—small engines simply require prior experience to start and regulate.

In my opinion, the most important safety tip is: "Slow down and use your brain." Just because the flag on a beach is green doesn't mean you are safe from drowning. Maybe you woke up feeling odd this morning and this is the first sign of an impending health emergency? No swim would be safe for you, not even the bathtub. Below are some further words of advice:

(1) Learn water safety (lifeguarding and First Aid): Plato believed that learning water safety is a virtue. OK, he probably never said that word-for-word, but using a syllogism from Aristotle, one can reason: Plato believed wisdom is a virtue. Learning water safety makes you wiser. Hence, Plato would call you virtuous if you learned water safety!

Swimmers should learn basic lifeguarding and First Aid principles, even if, at a bare minimum, this involves watching YouTube tips or just chatting with fellow swimmers who have taken the appropriate courses. After all, if the standard advice is to swim with a buddy, this raises the important question of how exactly one swimmer can help the other, avoiding the tragedy of the *two-buddy problem*: when one is drowning, the other does not know how to help safely, and the outcome is that both swimmers drown. This happens all too frequently because a panicked swimmer relentlessly grabs anything they can—in the process, even a child could drown an adult. William Shakespeare referred to the two-buddy problem at the beginning of *Macbeth*: "As two spent swimmers that do cling together, And choke their art." Lifeguarding lessons teach methods to avert this tragedy, and even offer solutions to the *three-buddy problem*: how does a third person approach the two-buddy drowning scenario and safely separate and rescue the two swimmers?

To find lifeguarding lessons in your region, search online for water safety organizations such as the Red Cross (www.redcross.org) and the Royal Life Saving Society (www.rlss.org.uk). I thought that lifeguarding lessons were extremely helpful, and I had a fun time during the classes as well. My goal was to be a well-prepared swimmer rather than to make a living as a lifeguard.

Other First Aid issues related to swimming tend to involve cuts and infections of the skin and ears. Ironically, my most common swim injuries are cuts to my feet when walking on rocks to enter or exit the water rather than anything that happens while I'm swimming. Bring gauze, antibiotic ointment, and treatments for ear problems. Note that pharmacies in Greece can supply these to tourists and the second language known by most Greeks is usually English.

Also, I highly recommend that a group of swimmers pause before they enter the water and disclose any potential health issues as well as their relevant health expertise. For example, I would mention that I am allergic to wasps and tell the others that I have an EpiPen injector in my bag on the beach. This way, my companions will be on alert for wasps, and if I am stung, they will know where to find the remedy. Others might share their possible health concerns and the actions to best help them. It would also be valuable to know who is trained in lifeguarding, First Aid, or works professionally in health fields.

Finally, I should note that one advantage to swimming in Crete as opposed to other, more remote islands is the availability of hospitals on the island, particularly in the major cities of the north coast. For the swimmers who worry about their proximity to hospital care, Crete is a good choice.

(2) Go / No Go, the danger of sticking to plans, and calling a swim: Safety begins before you enter the water, and much of it has to do with matters concerning the mind rather than the body. Usually, it's a good thing when you hear that a person is persistent, dependable, unwavering in their dedication, never late, ambitious, and someone who always achieves what they set out to do. However, these very same personality traits can lead to outcomes in open water swimming that are dangerous and even deadly.

In particular, I'm thinking of the person who has just five days in Crete, has set a goal to do one of the swims in this book, and has left it for the last day. What happens if, before they enter the water, a variety of factors are unexpectedly unfavorable? It could be that they are feeling a little light-headed that day for some mysterious reason. Or perhaps the wind is strong, and the forecast is for even stronger winds. Yet, because they need to achieve the goal they had set for themselves months ago—they've even told others about it—they get into the water anyway and tragedy strikes.

The greatest danger of all is to believe that *you would never be that person* who ignores warning signs when a swim is planned and about to begin. Unfortunately, the people who have perished are exactly like you and me. Take a look at one example where sticking to plans became deadly.

Eddie Would Go was written by Stuart Coleman and recounts how in 1978 a group in Hawaii planned a 4,000-km journey from Oahu to Tahiti in a Polynesian canoe called the *Hōkūleʻa* with no escort vessels. The idea was to achieve what the ancient Pacific Islanders had accomplished, using the stars at night for navigation. The start date for the journey was set months in advance, and the event was accompanied by speeches from the Governor of Hawaii and other political and cultural dignitaries. However, the weather conditions that day were bad and becoming worse. Nonetheless, they *stuck to plans* and departed the island of Oahu. The *Hōkūleʻa* capsized that same night and famed lifeguard and surfer Eddie Aikau drowned.

Coming to Crete for some swimming doesn't appear as newsworthy and high stakes as the fateful journey of the *Hōkūleʻa*. Yet, in the swimmer's mind there may be significant pressure and even incentives to do some of these swims at a specific time and day.

My advice is to always keep plans flexible because conditions may not be optimal. This flexibility *should continue* throughout the swim. To *"call a swim"* (canceling or stopping early) is not a failure. Instead, you should turn your attention to the joy of finding yourself in Crete in the first place and the simple pleasure of entering the water. In the long run, the island of Crete isn't going anywhere, and you can return some other day to finish what you set out to do in a safe and smart way.

Every swimmer can construct their own "Go / No Go Checklist" to review *before* every swim and even during a swim. Here is an example:

Go / No Go Checklist

- Am I fatigued or in pain from previous swims, a poor night's sleep, indigestion, migraines, or any other health developments?
- When I walk, then stop and bend down, do I feel dizzy or disoriented when I bring myself upright again?
- Am I hydrated?
- Am I coughing, short of breath, shivering, or feeling mentally foggy?
- Have I checked the weather forecast?

- Is my gear in good shape?
- Have I reviewed the maps and swim distances for the location?

(3) Paul's 50% Effort Rule: To help you overcome unforeseen problems, I highly recommend swimming at 50% of your maximum effort. Here are five reasons:

First, unsupervised coastal water swims do not have safety nets like escort boats or lifeguards on jet skis. Swimmers are entering a wild natural environment which has many unknowns in the present and a variety of changing conditions in the near future. Swimming at 50% effort preserves the extra strength that you might need when confronting difficult circumstances as they appear. For example, an unexpected change in conditions such as increased wind strength may severely challenge your physical ability to stay on course and return to the beach from which you started. Such conditions may blow you toward dangers you had planned to avoid, like ship traffic or a wave break. However, if you have physical energy held in reserve, you may be able to swim to safety.

Second, beginning a swim at 50% effort is also a sound strategy for sustaining a consistent pace. If you start at greater than 50% effort, you may become exhausted and not be able to finish your excursion. If you start at 50%, then you will more probably finish your swim and you'll be glad you didn't expend all your energy at the beginning. There is nothing to lose. If you find that starting at 50% was too easy, then you can always pick up the pace later.

Third, swimming at 50% provides a safety net for a greatly reduced breathing capacity due to ingesting or inhaling water and coughing. Just a few drops of swallowed or inhaled salt water can trigger coughing and this can make you feel like you have lost more than half of your lung capacity. Coughing for more than a few seconds can immediately exhaust the body. The perception that you cannot breathe or move can lead to a panic reaction that can worsen an already life-threatening situation. If you were already swimming near 100% effort, and you lose half your lung capacity due to a bout of coughing, then you may have to stop swimming to recover. Recovery may in fact be difficult, leading you down a path towards drowning. If you were following the 50% rule, then minor coughing can take place without stopping. In the worst case of swallowing a lot of water or coughing violently for an extended period of time, having that 50% buffer will allow you to recover more quickly and avoid the life-threatening scenario.

Fourth, the 50% rule helps when you must skip a breath due to oncoming choppy water. If you breathe every three strokes, you might occasionally skip a breath to avoid swallowing water had you opened your mouth. You may even rotate your head for the breath and then realize that you should keep your mouth closed. If you are swimming at 50% effort, skipping a breath should be easy, but if you are pushing yourself, then your options are reduced. You may be forced to breathe because you are out of air but end up with a mouthful of salt water instead.

Fifth, your safety may be threatened by an oncoming watercraft. If you have enough energy available for a 25-m sprint at 100% effort, that may make all the difference in the world when trying to avoid a collision.

How do you know you are swimming at 50% effort? Everyone is different, and even the same person may have a different level of physical fitness over time. I measure my 50% effort as the ability to change from breathing every three strokes to every five strokes for at least 10 seconds or being able to shallow dive underwater for 10 seconds and then continue swimming on the surface without stopping to recover my breath. In essence, *I am not gasping for air* while swimming—I always have the capacity to skip a breath if I choose to.

(4) Network with other people and groups: Recall that the standard advice is to avoid swimming alone. However, swimmers should network with other people who won't necessarily be swimming with them. If you are with friends or family, tell them the destination and duration of your swim. Before you start swimming, state the current time and when you expect to be back, e.g.: "It's now 1:30 pm. I should be back around 3:00 pm."

You may have calculated that you'll be back by 2:30 pm, but I recommend adding some extra time to what you communicate to others. You want to avoid "the danger of sticking to plans." If you end up needing extra time for your swim, you don't want to worry that friends and family will begin panicking about your safety. You may start making decisions that are incorrect, such as accelerating your pace to return "in time" when in fact you are physically unable to sustain the faster pace and end up exhausted in the water and requiring rescue. On the other hand, if you tackle a difficulty by finding the best solutions, which are not necessarily the fastest solutions, you may prevail with an excellent and safe swim, even if it took longer.

If you are on social media, posting a message on the Facebook group [Crete Open Water Swimming](#) announcing your swim plan might result in one or more members offering to drop by the beach to swim with you.

If you see a lifeguard, let them know about your swim plan too. Sometimes they will discourage open water swimming as their standard advice. In my experience, if you keep the conversation going, they will recognize that you are a skilled swimmer, and they will become more positive and helpful.

The people working at dive shops and rental equipment outlets are also very knowledgeable about local conditions. An easy conversation starter is to simply state that you want to go for a long swim and ask if they know the weather forecast for the day. They may also offer advice on other aspects of your swim, like a nice area to explore, or certain places to avoid. Sometimes they have photos or brochures that show the interesting local beaches and marine sites. You can always ask if these locations are swimmable, gauging their distances and directions.

Finally, you can join organized swim groups or paid tours (search the internet for "swimming holiday"), such as [SwimTrek](#) or [The Big Blue](#). I have not participated in these tours, but I do see these groups swimming at some of the locations described in my book. Because they offer the safety of guides and escort boats, they may have a wider repertoire of longer or more isolated swims. One idea is for you to spend a week with an organized swimming holiday, and then stay an extra few days, heading out on your own using my suggestions to explore swims in other parts of Crete. Perhaps by making new friends on the organized swimming tour, you will gain new swim buddies for my excursions.

(5) Always face the direction of danger: When swimming in breaking waves (surf), there is an important rule to never turn your back to the waves—your gaze and attention should be focused towards the oncoming waves. The swimmer needs to determine what type of wave is approaching and prepare for the encounter successfully. Generally, this means taking a deep breath and swimming forward and underneath the breaking wave (a "duck dive"). Even if there are no breaking waves, similar circumstances occur near rocks, in shallow water, or in marine caves. The waves or swells can push the swimmer straight into rock or coral.

Swimmers should practice facing the direction of danger so that it becomes instinctual. Under circumstances where you are physically tired or distracted, your brain may not remember this rule. So, the goal is to develop a default behavior of always turning towards oncoming waves no matter what your mental capacity happens to be.

Also, try not to spend too much time in these unpredictable areas. A dangerous location is not the best place to stop and adjust your goggles, for example. If possible, swim to a safer spot first and then adjust your goggles.

(6) Respect the sea: Many swimmers may have a weekly routine of swimming in a pool where every session is similar to the last, and the one before that. You are not thinking much about the future as you enter a pool. The pool water is there to serve your goals for recreation and sport. You are the master of that water.

In unsupervised open water swimming, nothing is guaranteed about your future and the sea is not there to serve your wishes and needs. Your mindset must change to that of a sailor, rather than a swimmer. Every minute and every hour you need to contemplate the situation presented before you in the water, respect the fact that you have no power to control conditions, and strive to achieve a harmony with the raw nature surrounding you. Of course, this is exactly what makes open water swimming so alluring!

(7) Identify emergency water exit points along your course: When I was learning to fly a plane, one lesson was to monitor the ground along a flight path for suitable areas to make an emergency landing (e.g., nearby fields and roads). The idea was to identify these spots before flying, and to keep looking for them while flying, rather than have the emergency strike first and then try to find them. So too, before you arrive at a beach, and certainly while swimming, you should scan for and keep a mental catalog of places to leave the water should an emergency require it. These water exit points could be other beaches along the course, but also climbable rocky areas protected from waves, and even anchored boats. Additionally, scan for exit points downwind of your intended course, since that is commonly the direction that people are pushed off course.

(8) Recognize the signs of drowning, hypothermia, and heat illnesses: There are any number of conditions—hyperthermia, hypothermia, cardiac arrest, shock, trauma, epileptic seizure, asthma attack, allergic reaction, etc.—that can weaken a person to the point where they drown. Drowning is defined as when submersion in water, even shallow water, cuts off respiration which could lead to death, injury, or recovery. The verb *drown* does not necessarily mean to die. A *passive* drowning victim is motionless with their face underwater without signs of breathing for roughly 30 seconds. Identifying an *active drowning* victim (one who is still breathing and conscious) is trickier because one might assume that they will be waving their hands above the water and calling for help. In fact, an active drowning victim may not exhibit any of these actions. Instead, they may look calm, with their mouth just above the water tilted upwards towards the sky, and with a vertical body position. One could also define a *distressed swimmer* as a person who is at an elevated risk of becoming an active drowning victim and it may be very difficult to distinguish the two.

Distressed swimmers and active drowning victims may be able to communicate and therefore a rescue attempt may involve talking to them first. If they can communicate, the rescuer needs to obtain consent to carry out a rescue. If they refuse help, their wish should be honored, but one could explain to them why they need help and the possible result if they do not accept it. They may change their mind.

If you find yourself gasping, coughing, and feeling highly anxious or panicked, then you may be a distressed swimmer on the path to drowning. **You can signal for help by waving one arm high above the water**, but you would also need to find ways to relax, float, and breathe. All swimmers should practice techniques to relax in the water, even if you think you would never be that person who drowns. If you practice now, then later, when you find yourself gasping and panicking, you will be able to remember your training and be confident that relaxing is something you can achieve. Such techniques include controlling your breath (breathing in slowly and exhaling slowly) and calming your thoughts and feelings (see the next section).

Hypothermia (dangerously low body temperature) is rather tricky because it affects your brain and clouds your judgement. This means that even if under normal circumstances you know that shivering and chattering teeth are signs of hypothermia, your mind in the water will not recognize these signs or have the capacity to make safe decisions.

In addition to shivering, memory loss, and confusion, signs of hypothermia include slurred speech, drowsiness, fatigue, slow and shallow breathing, and uncoordinated movement. Two ways to self-assess for hypothermia are to test your memory and speech. For example, test your memory by figuring out what day it was three days ago. The answer requires remembering the name of the present day and how that translates to three days prior. If you are surprised that you cannot accomplish this task, it is best to head straight to the nearest point where you can exit the water and warm up (assuming it is a sunny, calm, and warm day). To test if your speech is slurring, stop swimming and try to recite a song or a story out loud, e.g., "Once upon a time…"

If a swimmer cannot make it to shore (additional swimming can worsen the hypothermia), they need to slow the heat loss. They can cross their arms over their chest, keep their head above the water, hug a swim buddy, put on a swim cap, and move to warmer water (shallow and still areas are often warmest).

Heat-related illnesses in order of increasing severity include heat cramps (muscle spasms in the arms, legs, and abdomen), heat exhaustion (elevated body temperature, headache, nausea, dizziness, confusion, weakness, thirst, irritability), and heat stroke (very high body temperature, slurred speech, headache, confusion, hot skin, sweating, rapid or shallow breathing and pulse, vomiting, seizures, unconsciousness). Stopping a swim, resting in a cool environment, and drinking water are obvious responses, and everyone should guard against dehydration and sunburn. Many health emergencies in Greece over the summer are heat related and as swimmers we are in a deceptive situation of exerting ourselves physically, yet the signs of overheating may not be obvious in the water. Also, if you are not originally from a hot climate, visitors to Crete during the summer have a higher risk of heat-related health emergencies.

(9) Practice CPR Thoughts for anxiety and panic: To prepare for anxiety or panic attacks, readers can practice **Coping, Power,** and **Reward** (CPR) ***Thoughts***. This is my psychological version of CardioPulmonary Resuscitation used on the heart and lungs. Examples of *coping thoughts* are: "this fear will pass," "just breath and relax," "I'm OK," "I trust my skills," and, "one thing at a time." Concentrate also on relaxing the body, face, neck, shoulder, and arms. A *power thought* is more assertive and commanding, such as, "I am doing everything in my power to be safe," "I have always controlled my fear," and "I know how to float, and I can overcome anything that comes my way." A *reward thought* displaces attention and emotion from the present difficulty by *visualizing* a future benefit, such as, "When I am done with this, I am going to that shop on the beach to order *three* scoops of ice cream." Swimmers should practice CPR Thoughts when they are doing comfortable swims. Then, when a difficult situation demands it, use the same CPR Thoughts to crowd out any anxiety or panic thoughts. Anxiety is defined as a constant worry and a hopeless feeling that there is no way to manage the worry. A panic attack has more intense physical symptoms (but with a shorter duration compared to anxiety), including difficulty breathing, shaking, and a rapid heart rate, which can cause a person to feel like they are dying. In general, it is important to pay attention to your thoughts, which invoke feelings, since both thoughts and feelings can lead to incorrect decisions.

(10) Look out for potentially dangerous marine life: For surface swimming, the good news is that jellyfish are rare along the coastal areas of Crete. Perhaps the most common danger is stepping on a sea urchin. This will probably not create an emergency health crisis, but later you may have to soften your skin with water and try to pick out the spines using tweezers or a needle that has been sterilized. Some may be impossible to remove, and you can join me in being part human, part sea urchin. Also, exploring dark, rocky areas runs the risk of encountering the invasive **lionfish**. They will not come out to attack you, yet they won't swim away either when you approach them. Thus, you may be stung if you accidentally collide with them swimming through a dark tunnel or diving underwater. This motivates my recommendation to swim with clear-lens goggles in order to have the best vision possible. A sting will require the swimmer to return to shore calmly and quickly to monitor for any symptoms that may develop. The recommendation is to remove the stinger if it is still lodged in the skin and then apply heat locally (e.g., a hot cup of tea or a stone warmed by the sun) for at least 30 minutes to break down the venom. As with any puncture wound, you should also clean it, apply pressure to stop bleeding, and use an antibiotic ointment.

(11) Dive through tunnels cautiously and conservatively, have a buddy too: This book describes places to swim into caves and one cave may connect to a neighboring cave or have a second outlet to the sea via a short tunnel. These tunnels may be entirely submerged or have a low ceiling above the water. If you have the fitness and air capacity to complete a tunnel passage, it is vital to protect your head from hitting any rock. If the water is too turbulent or wavy for you to control your motion, simply skip the tunnel. Do not do it.

Even under favorable conditions, the buoyancy of the salt water or the reflex to move up towards the surface when the air in your lungs seems depleted can also cause you to hit your head on the rock above. You may not even realize you are moving up. It can be hard to look up, and when you do, you will likely move up accidentally. Try to be aware of your depth by looking down at the seafloor or by noting rocky landmarks to the sides. Swim farther forward than the point where you think you should start your ascent to the surface, and when you do begin to rise, place one hand above your head. Despite your precautions, you may have made a mistake and started an ascent too early with rock still above you. If you do hit your head, you may need assistance. If you have a swim buddy, there is a chance they can pull you out. One buddy should serve as a spotter for the other: swim through dangerous areas one at a time.

(12) Assume others are blind: For all practical purposes, a swimmer is invisible to watercraft, and this can be true even if you have the most glaringly red swim cap and buoy. Consider that pilots of watercraft may be looking out for swimmers within 100 m of shore, and possibly up to 200 or 300 m. But from 400 m and beyond, they are looking out for other watercraft and would not expect to encounter a swimmer. If you are swimming in the low season for tourism (October–May), then they may not expect to find a swimmer *anywhere* in the water. Though you exist in the water, if the other person is not tuning their vision and attention to see you, then you will be invisible. Psychologists call this inattentional blindness.

A related example is that you cannot be seen if the sun is low in the sky and the pilot is literally blinded, no matter what their state of attention happens to be. Thus, **if you are swimming with sunset to your left, you should assume you are invisible to watercraft coming from the right**, even under completely flat water conditions.

One final example concerns taking action when a person is drowning in close proximity to many other people. It may be hard to believe that you are witnessing a drowning because surely the other people right next to the victim can see it and would have done something already. What are they, blind? Yes. On the one hand they may not have the training to recognize a drowning person, and on the other hand, they may not be paying attention to their immediate environment. If you assume they are blind, then you will be faster in taking action to rescue the person.

(13) Test yourself first in a safer environment: Physical fitness on land does not automatically translate to fitness in the water. I have gone swimming with friends who seem to be aerobically fit enough to run a marathon, climb Everest, or join an elite military unit, yet 50 m of swimming is slow and has them gasping for air. Exhausted people in open water can drown and die. The illusion of a fitness crossover from land to water is rather dangerous. I would recommend that everyone tests themselves in pools or in shallow open-water areas with short swims before trying the longer ones. With practice, many will be able to do the longer swims, but it would be a mistake to dive right in. The same is true for those who swam a lot last year, but not so much in the past few months. Test yourself first, find out what is easy and what is hard, and then consider your options before you try the swims in this book. So too, any planned night swim should be rehearsed thoroughly during the daytime.

Gear

To enjoy my swimming excursions safely, I can offer a few basic suggestions on equipment. This is not a thorough list with detailed descriptions, but I hope it inspires readers to explore their options further by searching for additional articles and product reviews. Note that swimming in the sea can be significantly rougher than a pool, requiring more rugged and specialized gear. Therefore, in addition to a generic sporting goods store, one might explore places that sell items for scuba diving, boating, fishing, and the various surfing-related sports.

Goggles: I think that having clear-lens goggles in like-new condition is the number one item for safe and enjoyable swimming. Being able to see in front and around you both in the water and out is essential for avoiding threats and clearly perceiving navigation cues. Nevertheless, some people enjoy swimming *without* goggles, finding them uncomfortable, limiting their vision, or simply unnecessary. Indeed, a key problem is finding comfortable goggles for your unique face—one size does not fit all. Here are a few more things to take into consideration:

- To find goggles that are unlikely to leak, the classic test is to press the lenses against your eye sockets (without wrapping the strap behind your head), and if the suction keeps them on your face for a moment, then that is a good fit. However, if the goggles blur your vision or cause discomfort around the eye socket and over the nose, choose a different pair.
- I use the same goggles in open water as in the pool. Racing or training goggles have a small profile and the forces from breaking waves or wind-driven chop are similar to diving in a pool or pushing off a wall. Under these conditions, larger goggles or masks will be ripped from your face, leak or you will need to make them uncomfortably tight to keep them on. Smaller goggles will stay on without as much tightening of the strap. In calm conditions any goggles or masks that are comfortable for you will work fine.
- Lenses for goggles and sunglasses can be mirrored, tinted, and polarized to reduce the brightness and change the color of light. All lenses block UV wavelengths. Blue-*tinted* lenses *transmit* blue light and make the world appear bluer. Blue-*mirrored* lenses *block* blue light and make the world appear warmer, improving the perception of contrast. Gray-tinted ("smoke") or silver-mirrored lenses decrease brightness without changing color. Some lenses are mirrored and color tinted so that the tint determines the color. Glare is the whitening of a scene due to sunlight. Sunlight bouncing off various things becomes polarized and at certain viewing angles only polarized lenses can selectively diminish this type of glare as well as darken a blue sky. Blue-tinted or orange-mirrored lenses darken a blue sky in every direction. Near sunset or sunrise, orange-tinted or blue-mirrored lenses help brighten a scene given the warmer solar color.
- All goggles will magically disappear from your face, never to be found again, as you swim out through breaking waves. It is best to have your goggles tucked inside your swimsuit until you get past the surf. Or you can put on your goggles first, and then wear your swim cap over the goggle strap.

- The most convenient anti-fog coating is your own saliva that you spit into the goggles and possibly rinse once before wearing them. One can also use diluted baby shampoo. Some goggles have a boxier shape than others which lets a small pool of water sit inside the bottom corner away from the eye while swimming (larger masks allow this too). One can occasionally tilt the head to make this water run across the lens and clear away the fog.
- Avoid touching the goggle lenses if your hands have sunscreen, Vaseline, or other oily substances on them.
- I bring two pairs of goggles to the beach just in case one of them is lost or damaged. Some people also swim with a backup pair of goggles. I find that goggles do not unexpectedly break or start leaking if I have been using them day after day successfully. For very long swims, I might bring an extra pair of different-style goggles that allows me to change where the pressure is placed on my eye sockets and head.
- On a fixed budget, I would rather buy inexpensive goggles frequently than incur the equivalent cost in expensive goggles less frequently. Most new goggles with an anti-fog feature will give a few weeks of great performance.
- Salt water is abrasive, particularly if it dries on the lenses. Try rinsing or soaking goggles with fresh water frequently. In general, one should expect a shorter goggle lifetime in salt water compared to freshwater swimming.

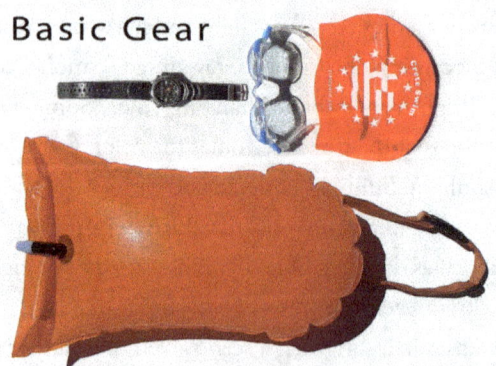

Swim Cap: Wearing a swim cap is a necessity for those swimmers with long hair but may seem optional for short-haired people. Yet there are many reasons for everyone to wear a swim cap. From a safety perspective, a swim cap makes the swimmer slightly more visible, it protects the head from direct sunshine, it slows heat loss that can lead to hypothermia, and it protects the scalp from lesions when the head collides with someone else's foot, floating debris, or the unforgiving rock when swimming in tunnels and caves. A bright (e.g., red) color is recommended to maximize visibility to vessels, other swimmers, and people on shore. A white cap is the same color as water chop and would only help in calm waters.

However, wearing a bright cap could also be dangerous if it gives a swimmer a false sense of security. They may be thinking, "Surely that jet ski coming my way can see my flaming red swim cap and won't run straight into me, right?" Wrong! The cap may go unnoticed and does NOT prevent that accident from happening.

Another good reason to wear a cap is that it identifies you as an open water swimmer. A lifeguard may be less likely to worry that you are swimming out of sight, a fellow open water swimmer who is looking for a swim buddy might approach you to swim together, or someone who is knowledgeable about the area might come and give you advice before you get in.

Silicone caps are thicker and warmer compared to latex, while some prefer fabric. Neoprene is the warmest for winter swimming. I would recommend bringing two caps to the beach in case one tears. Finally, when swimming as a group, those designated as the guides could wear a different colored cap (or swim buoy), so that they can be identified in the water by the other swimmers.

Wristwatch: The first invention in human history to kick off the "quantified-self movement" was the wrist or pocket watch. People have learned to quantify just about everything, from how much faster or slower they travel on any given day, to how long they sleep and work. For open water swimming, I often wear a rugged Citizen dive watch to monitor my swim time between points. In subsequent chapters I provide the approximate *distances* of swim routes, but these do not directly translate to how much *time* you will spend in the water. The wind and waves will change your speed. Open water swim times are generally slower than pool times, and you may pause frequently to explore the beautiful marine world or take rest breaks. Therefore, you need a watch to keep track of time.

For example, imagine I decided to keep my total swim time under two hours to safeguard against exhaustion, hypothermia, dehydration, sunburn, or cramping. Also, my friends on the beach are planning to leave in two hours. If I find that it took me 45 minutes to swim to a location with the wind behind me, and realize that it will take me longer to return against the wind, then I need to begin returning immediately if I am to keep my total swim time safely under two hours.

Many dive or open water watches are expensive, but as long as you have something waterproof that tells time on your wrist, even if it is a cheaper purchase, you will gain fundamental information that is handy (pun intended) for your swim. Note that GPS-enabled watches are not a basic need for the swims in this book. Nevertheless, I enjoy using them to record my routes and understand how to best follow my intended courses. Swimmers who wish to have an added safety net could also purchase a personal locator beacon (there are many varieties).

Swim Buoy (tow float): A personal swim buoy is **necessary for visibility** on the water and offers many other safety advantages and conveniences. In winds below five Beaufort and in non-wavy conditions, I have found that:

- A swim buoy does not impede my swim—e.g., it does not interfere with my swim kick—in most situations.
- It can aid in the swim because I will spend less time arching my head high above the water to check if watercraft can see me. Instead, I can streamline my swim for more time as if I were in a lap pool.
- It advertises a level of aquatic professionalism with at least two important effects: (1) lifeguards and passing boats are less likely to interrupt my swim to check if I am a lost or distressed, and (2) it conveys a message to other recreational swimmers that swimming away from the shallow or protected areas of the beach requires preparation.
- I can use a buoy to rest and relax. A small buoy serves as a neck pillow when I float on my back.
- A buoy may have a "dry" compartment to transport money, sunscreen, mobile phones, car keys, footwear, water, snacks, etc. Note that water tends to leak into a buoy's pocket and a second layer of protection is recommended. For example, I would place a mobile phone in a small waterproof pouch, and then place the pouch in the buoy's compartment.
- Some buoys have a transparent side pocket intended for cell phone use, but one can also insert a small LED light for night swims and caves.

- A buoy could also carry a sound source for visually impaired swimmers to follow a guide swimmer.
- When encountering a swimmer in distress, handing over your buoy could help them. Note that personal swim buoys are not meant to be lifesaving devices, lacking the necessary ruggedness, buoyancy, and design.
- If the swimmer's arms need a rest, they can hold the buoy in front of them (like a kickboard) and kick to keep moving forward.
- If a group of swimmers spreads out beyond 40 m diameter, it can be difficult for them to see each other. Buoys are great for keeping track of everyone.
- Buoys allow a group of swimmers with varying abilities to attempt a challenging swim together more safely.

Even with all these advantages, it's important to note that a personal swim buoy can be problematic in high winds or in wavy conditions. When swimming against high winds or waves, the buoy produces extra drag, and if you change directions relative to the wind and waves, the line that connects the buoy to your body may get tangled around your legs. I have had buoys blown all the way in front of me when the wind was gusting at my back. One solution is to partially deflate the buoy, which increases its drag on the water, but decreases how easily it is blown around. The buoy should be completely deflated when entering and exiting the sea with breaking waves. In these more extreme conditions, smaller-sized buoys (15 liters or less) will be easier to handle than larger ones. On the other hand, given boat traffic and a choppy sea, a larger buoy has higher visibility. **One might even stop swimming to lift the buoy above the water to help nearby vessels notice you.** Finally, note that swimmers can also use floats and boards meant for spearfishing and scuba diving. These allow the installation of a more visible flag and can be weighted down in windy conditions. I use the Cressi Spearfishing Signal Board Buoy which has a safety whistle, flag, and storage.

Fins: Fins are definitely allowed, as are diving masks and snorkels—this is swimming tourism, not a race. For a group of people with varying abilities, the slower swimmers could use fins to keep up with the faster ones. Or, if you are capable enough for short swims, fins can help with the much longer swims. Another scenario is that you planned to swim in Crete day after day for a week—

something you don't normally do back home—and by the third day you are tired. Fins could help you continue your swims safely after spending the first few days without them. In a similar vein, if you have suffered a recent upper body injury, fins can help ease the strain of swimming. If you arrive in Crete with no fins and then decide you need them, there are plenty of shops in villages and near beaches that will have the snorkeling models. It will be harder to find the more specialized, shorter-blade swimming fins used for training, but there are sporting goods stores in the larger cities like Chania, Rethymno, and Heraklion that will carry them. Before going on a long swim with new fins, I would suggest a few short outings first to test for skin blistering and muscle cramping.

Mobile Phone: Salt water kills devices—this is Poseidon's favorite power that the ancient Greeks forgot to warn us about! In fact, one of humankind's first devices was invented by the ancient Greeks —it's called the [Antikythera mechanism](#)—but it was lost at sea 30 km northwest of Crete over two thousand years ago and rediscovered in 1901. The Greeks wanted to use it as a GPS to calculate their position relative to the Moon, Sun, and stars. Instead, it became the first device taken by [Poseidon](#), and he still loves destroying the devices of mere mortals.

Many phones are ostensibly "waterproof" but floating pouches can be used to tow your mobile phone while swimming. In addition to taking photos, using the GPS function and maps, or the LED light in darkness, a mobile phone adds a layer of safety if you have a cellular signal and need to make an emergency call (dial 112). As noted above, a phone can be placed within a swim buoy but a second layer of protection, such as a clear food storage bag that seals, is recommended.

Swimwear: Like the situation with goggles, what you choose to wear is a highly personal decision. The swimsuit that I wear in open water is the same as what I use for pool workouts. However, I look for swimsuits with a small pocket to store waterproof action cameras, coins, and keys.

For those who feel uncomfortable wearing the stretchy and form-fitting competition swimwear, try to find "board shorts" (as in surfboards). These are worn by surfers, windsurfers, kite surfers, etc., and have a tight cut around the waist and thigh (as opposed to baggy and loose), which minimizes drag. Board shorts are usually made of material that is durable and does not absorb much water, drying out rather fast. Occasionally I will wear board shorts for long distance swims and feel very comfortable, barely perceiving the extra drag.

For me, the water in Crete seems warm enough during the summer that I do not need to wear a wetsuit for swims of up to two hours, yet others may desire it. Many people may wish to protect their back and shoulders from the sun by wearing a rash guard. However, if this causes excessive skin chafing, the cost may outweigh the benefit.

Action Cameras, Flashlight, and Keys: I often swim with an action camera on a thin selfie stick that I run through the side of my swimsuit. Yes, this creates extra drag in the water, but for me the benefit of having an underwater camera outweighs the cost of the extra swimming effort. Another option is to tow a thicker, floating selfie stick with its wrist strap attached to the waist belt of the swim buoy. Afterwards, I recommend submerging cameras in fresh water for one hour to dissolve the salt crystals rather than simply rinsing them.

A waterproof flashlight is needed if you intend to explore the darkest part of a marine cave. As you float slowly forward, you can check underwater for obstructions and sea life that you should avoid disturbing, such as lionfish and shrimp. Shining the light above the water will reveal the geological features of the cave as well as any birds or bats.

How to deal with a car key is also worth thinking about. I tie my car key to the string of my swimsuit's waistband, but one needs to figure out if the key is waterproof or not. One trick for many electronic key fobs involves removing a tiny manual key, locking the larger electronic fob in the car, and swimming with the manual key tied to your swimsuit. If this option is not available, one needs to either hide the electronic key fob somewhere on land or bring it along in a waterproof pouch. As noted above, one major reason to use a buoy is to swim with your valuables such as car keys.

Preparation

Some of my recommended swims can be accomplished by anyone who is comfortable floating in water and capable of an easy-going breaststroke. They don't even need goggles or a swim cap. However, most of the swims require some practice in a safe environment such as a swimming pool or shallow areas near beaches. Also, it never hurts to train with a coach or a more experienced swimmer to improve your technique, strength, and endurance. With that said, I also believe that if you've found a swim stroke and exercise routine that seem to work well for you from age 5 and onward to age 105, with minimal interruptions due to injuries, then you're doing just fine. You be you! Here are a few more ideas on how to prepare for your swimming holiday in Crete:

Practice physical and mental relaxation: Everyone is different and must be responsible for giving honest thought to their own physical and mental abilities. As noted in the introduction, it's hard to "know thyself." Physical and mental fitness on land does not automatically convert to fitness in the water. Just the mental component is significantly different. After all, if you run a marathon, you can always flop down on the ground exhausted, but when a swimmer does that in the water, we call that drowning.

The swimmer's mind must be calm, disciplined, dispassionate, and attentive at all times. Practicing relaxation is extremely important and involves attention to changing your mental and physical state. Here are just a few suggestions:

- When your face is in the water during your stroke, exhale a few bubbles of air continuously rather than strain to hold your breath completely. This will relax tension in your chest and abdomen. (Holding a breath depletes energy because it mostly fights the need to exhale air rather than inhale air.)
- Change to a more relaxing stroke, such as a light breaststroke or backstroke.
- If looking at the open sea is frightening, direct your gaze and attention to the shoreline, even to the extent of abandoning bilateral breathing for the comfort of sighting in the direction of shore. Or change to a sidestroke or breaststroke that allows you to spend more time looking at land. Try smiling happily too.
- To reign in racing thoughts that flood your mind, practice the CPR Thoughts (Coping, Power, and Reward) discussed earlier, or try counting your stroke cycles or breaths.
- Stop swimming, float, and practice at least a minute of controlled breathing, exhaling and inhaling slowly and steadily. Try breathing by expanding your belly instead of your chest.

- Float on your back, close your eyes, and direct your gaze upwards towards your eyebrows. Become attentive to any sounds you can hear for a minute or two. Next, mentally scan your entire body and think about relaxing each area, including your facial muscles. End by smiling peacefully at the sun.
- Start learning these techniques in the deep end of a swimming pool or in shallow, protected open water areas.

Remember, even if you *never* need to use these suggestions yourself, it helps to learn them as handy tools to help another swimmer in distress.

Measure your ability: Even though I will provide approximate distances for each swim route, swimmers need to know how a distance translates to their personal time and effort. The basic number to measure is the average 100-m time over a much larger total distance (e.g., 400 m or more) at 50% effort (i.e., not gasping for air). This can be further parsed into 100-m times for calm vs. choppy conditions, short vs. long courses, with fins vs. without fins, etc. All of this helps in predicting the total swim time for a given distance (which should be communicated to non-swimmers as a safety precaution) and whether a swim could be unsafe. It also greatly assists swim leaders in planning group swims.

For example, in a pool you might measure 1 min, 40 sec as your average 100-m time at 50% effort. Open water swimming is slower by roughly 15%, so you would estimate a pace of 100 m every two minutes. Given a 1-km roundtrip course, you would plan to be in the water for 20 minutes without rest breaks. You might tell someone on the beach that you will be gone for 30 minutes just for the sake of providing an extra 10-minute allowance for resting and sightseeing. Or, if you were to join a new swim group, you could tell the leader your swim pace and then be assigned swim buddies of similar ability. Very broadly speaking, an open water swim pace of two minutes or less per 100 m is above average.

Another measurement worth making is counting the number of stroke cycles needed to go a certain distance. For example, swimming the length of a 50-m pool might require 30 freestyle stroke cycles (every time the right hand enters the water counts as one cycle). This knowledge is useful in open water when you start getting tired and wish to insert periodic rest breaks as a coping strategy. If 500 m remain at the end of a swim, this distance can be broken up into five 100-m segments. With every 60 stroke cycles, you will cover roughly 100 m and can stop and rest.

Improve sighting with head-up freestyle (front crawl): Unsupervised open water swims involve looking forward, navigating towards your destination, checking the position, direction, and velocity of boat traffic, swimming through tunnels, caves, channels, and breaking waves, keeping track of other swimmers, scanning for marine life, and generally having fun sightseeing above and below the water surface. Some coaches for open water swimming may advise against looking forward because it is tiring: it angles the body so that the legs drop downward when the head comes up, causing drag, and it strains the neck and back. However, these coaches may be supervising the swims, often with an escort vessel, which means that they are doing the important work of keeping the swimmers on course and protecting them from threats.

If you are on your own, it is up to you to do these jobs and I would recommend sighting forward by periodically tilting your head up at the moment one of your arms enters the water in front of you. One or more stroke cycles can take place with your eyes above the water. This might cause strain, but it is worth the benefits of swimming on course and avoiding collisions with other things in the sea. Note that the mouth does not necessarily rise above the water since you can still take a breath a moment later sideways.

In the photos above—"Say Cheese!" and "Then Breathe"—one can imagine snapping a quick selfie by looking forward at a camera with your eyes just above the water, then turning your head quickly to take a breath. I recommend sighting for the amount of time it takes to imagine speaking the words "say cheese"—this is how much time you need to properly recognize features in your field of view.

Swimmers who tend to swim in arcs or circles should definitely try sighting forward every three or four breaths. In the photos I am swimming through a rocky tunnel at Spilies Beach (swim #4) which requires sighting forward once every few breaths.

Two more things to keep in mind are: (1) Just as the eyes come up to sight forward (Say Cheese!), give a little extra power to your kick to avoid sinking the lower half of your body. (2) When you turn your head to breathe, your ear may be exposed to water chop slapping up against it. If this becomes a problem, tilt your head down after you sight forward, tucking your chin towards your chest as you simultaneously rotate to take a breath, keeping the ear safely underwater.

Sighting forward with head-up freestyle is also a basic rescue skill. If you are swimming toward someone who is drowning, you must keep an eye on them because if they go permanently below the surface you need to know exactly where to swim and dive to retrieve them.

Focus on the kick: A steady freestyle flutter kick is needed in open water swimming for a variety of reasons. As noted above, a head-up freestyle will sink the lower half of your body and a stronger kick compensates for that. In choppy conditions, you may have difficulty using your arms efficiently, but a strong kick will serve as a constant source of propulsion. In narrow areas between rocks or in tunnels, your arms may have limited clearance to accomplish a stroke. Again, a strong kick is needed for propulsion. In narrow channels with waves, you may need your arms to compensate for unwanted motions towards the rocks, but your kick will still provide forward motion. The same is true when diving forward to get through a breaking wave—the arms will pause, typically leaving one arm straight out in front while the kick continues. Finally, lap pool swimmers will be accustomed to pushing off the wall to establish forward momentum and then engaging the arms for propulsion. In open water, there is no wall to initiate movement and it can be strenuous if the effort comes from the arms alone. I would recommend starting with a strong kick (which can be a breaststroke kick) as you execute your first stroke so that the arms do not bear all the strain in overcoming your inertia of rest. Note that a freestyle kick originates from the hips, with minimal bending of the knees.

Master an effortless eggbeater: Treading water (floating in a vertical position) is needed in open water swimming when you are adjusting your goggles, checking the area around you for threats, searching for other swimmers, figuring out navigation markers, talking to other swimmers, taking photos, or simply resting. Using a breaststroke or freestyle kick to tread water is inefficient. Instead, the "eggbeater kick" involves rotating your lower legs in circles like an eggbeater. Your thighs may be raised, almost as if sitting in a chair. Given buoyant salt water, a gentle eggbeater should keep you afloat and it should not be exhausting. However, you need to practice relaxing so that the eggbeater seems effortless. Your breathing and heart rate should resemble the rest state. If you practice in the pool first, then later in salt water it will seem easier and psychologically reassuring that you can float vertically with a very light eggbeater and minimal arm motion. In a pool, you can remain stationary, or you can try moving back and forth from wall to wall. Try not to use your arms and focus on calming down and slowing your breath. You can make it more challenging by raising your hands so that they are just above the surface of the water. For a workout that will be anything but restful, do laps with the eggbeater kick and put your hands on top of your head.

Practice different strokes: Being able to swim at least one other stroke in addition to freestyle is important for a variety of health and safety reasons. Freestyle uses certain muscle groups which can suffer extreme fatigue, and an injury or cramp can disable a swimmer. Reverting to a different stroke can give those freestyle muscles a break. While breaststroke and backstroke readily come to mind, I also recommend working on your sidestroke, which relies on a scissor kick. Other than varying the muscles used, the sidestroke is needed when one arm is disabled or when towing something. For example, if you need to rescue someone, one arm could tow them while your other arm reaches forward for the stroke. The breaststroke, sidestroke, and backstroke are also useful for having your face out of the water. This may be needed when sighting, searching for something, or to lessen the feeling of anxiety or panic. For instance, the sidestroke allows you to fix your gaze on the coastline when swimming parallel to shore.

Use bilateral breathing: Swimming is a unique activity in that it functionally links your eyes to your mouth: what you see depends on how you breathe. In open water swimming what you can or cannot see is incredibly important, and therefore how you breathe is even more important than with pool swimming. I would highly recommend learning and practicing two-sided or *bilateral breathing*. Generally, this means taking breaths on both sides of your body over time. Breathing every odd number of strokes will accomplish this, but one could take several breaths in a row on one side, then take several breaths on the other.

Bilateral breathing balances the upper body muscles being used and in open water swimming allows the swimmer to scan for navigation cues and threats to the left and right. If one breathes only on one side (one-sided breathing or unilateral breathing), then an open water swimmer is blind to the other side, may not be able to swim a straight course, and may be more susceptible to muscle fatigue and damage such as shoulder impingement. Thus, when a person is in a pool or in easy open water conditions, this is a great time to practice bilateral breathing.

However, there are many reasons to revert to one-sided breathing. The most common reason is exhaustion from physical effort—one needs to take a breath more frequently. Also, the weather may be hitting you on one side, so that the opposite (downwind) side becomes the preferred place to open your mouth to breathe. If you revert to one-sided breathing in open water, it is important to more frequently check progress on your course and search for threats by either sighting forward or stopping to scan around you.

An overarching reason to practice bilateral breathing is to instill physical and mental discipline and planning. Swimming is a rather amazing activity because every breath is a plan. If you are running, you can breathe whenever you like. In swimming, you need to plan how your breath right now is going to play out in the future. This requires taking a breath that is sufficient to get you to the next breath, but also controlling your mental and physical state while holding that very same breath. Such discipline is the foundation to responding to other threats and stressors. When you are good at bilateral breathing, you will also be better at breathing calmly when you need to hold your breath longer than expected or when you are emotionally distraught by changing circumstances.

Assess and practice underwater endurance while keeping calm: Several swims are along coastlines with caves and underwater tunnels. If you wish to dive through a tunnel, it's critical to know your breath-holding capacity beforehand. In a pool or shallow open water, you can test how far you can swim underwater. You may find that you've overestimated your abilities and that could spell disaster. Or you may realize that you can swim much farther than you expected and that will open up all kinds of new opportunities. Whichever the case, you should be able to increase your underwater swimming capacity with practice. In particular, try to be graceful, unhurried, and calm while swimming underwater.

Differences between lap pool and open water swimming:

Walls vs. No Walls: Turns at the ends of pool lanes allow swimmers to propel themselves with their legs pushing off the wall, giving the arms a momentary rest, and briefly picking up speed with the push. Without the pool wall, the arms are *always working* until you decide to rest. **The net effect is that swimming in open water *without* walls is *slower* than in the pool by 10–30%.** Therefore, when you look at a map and see a 1-km swim that in the pool might take you 18 minutes, you should calculate 20 minutes or more in open water under ideal conditions.

Since the arms are working continuously in open water swimming, I also recommend varying parts of your stroke or changing to a different stroke to use different muscle groups and joint motions over time. Breaststroke is helpful because it is the only stroke where the arm does not travel over the head; the other strokes require a greater range of motion that can strain the shoulders.

In freestyle (front crawl) you have a choice on how far in front of your head the hands enter the water and how far forward you reach (extend) for the *glide*, just before you *catch* the water and *pull* backwards. If you reach forward as far as possible you will feel the muscles of the back and abdomen more engaged in the underwater pull, taking some of the workload off the shoulders and arms. But if the hands enter the water closer to your head with little or no glide, then you will have a shorter and faster stroke that focuses more work on the shoulders and arms. If you alternate between these two different hand-entry points and glide distances, you will not be working any one muscle group at maximum effort all the time.

Also, I recommend **taking breaks to improve the quality of your swim**. Your muscles will become fatigued with continuous swimming and your stroke will become sloppy, less effective, and possibly lead to injury or water ingestion. If you pause your swimming, perhaps stretch a bit, and then restart, you will naturally reboot to a better swim technique.

Distance vs. Time: Elaborating on the concept above, note that in a pool swim one can reliably convert a distance to a time interval (e.g., 1 km requires 18 minutes). However, in open water, if we see a 1-km range between two reference points, such as the beach and an island, then this information alone does not give us a time. Clearly our time will depend on whether we are swimming with or against the prevailing winds, in addition to the 10–30% slower pace due to the absence of walls, and the fact that our heading may be pointing away from our destination (see Marine Navigation in Chapter 1). Distance does not directly translate to time in open water swimming.

Sweet vs. Salty: Small amounts of pool water in your mouth or ingested is practically unnoticeable to many people. Even if pool water triggers a coughing fit, it's easy to stop swimming and rest, or climb out of the pool altogether. However, salt water, even a tiny quantity that enters the mouth *without* being ingested, can trigger coughing or a shortness of breath. The open water swimmer must be more vigilant about taking in water—the Mediterranean is salty! A coughing fit may be stronger and last longer than anything you have experienced in the pool, and this will deplete your energy and cause mental distress. Even though salt water is more buoyant, a panicking swimmer may not be able to relax in a way that is needed to float. Try to remain calm and float until the coughing passes. In more extreme cases of breathing significant amounts of salt water into the lungs, one's blood pressure may fall quickly and lead to shock. Even small amounts of sea water aspirated into the lungs may still lead to medical problems (e.g., dyspnea; a persistent shortness of breath) requiring a visit to the hospital.

Looking Down AND Up: To swim straight in lap pools, we look *under* the water for the navigation cues provided by markings on the floor and walls, and to our sides at the lane lines. These nearby reference points are called *proximal* cues. In the sea, most navigation cues are *distal* (distant), lying *above* the water level, such as the coastline, islands, buoys, anchored boats, trees, mountains, buildings, etc. Swimming straight will require attention to these distal cues by sighting frequently and bilateral breathing. Proximal cues could be other swimmers and the sea bottom. Underwater landmarks can be useful for gauging time or distance traveled rather than a direction. For example, on the outbound leg one might see a patch of seaweed 20 minutes into the swim. Later, as soon as the swimmer spots that seaweed again on the return leg they would know that roughly 20 minutes remain in their swim.

A pool exercise that can improve straight-line swimming is one-armed freestyle. Choose an arm and point it straight out, making your entire body like an arrow pointing to the other side, as if you were a lane line yourself. Then use your other hand for the freestyle stroke. This will require a stronger kick, a shorter glide, and frequent breaths to the side or forward (one can also hold a kickboard in front). Alternate which hand does the stroke every lap or half-lap. This exercise trains the brain to have a stronger sense of what self-motion in a straight line feels like (*proprioception*) because you see your arm pointing straight out ahead of you.

Lastly, looking down at the seafloor helps gauge the speed and direction of the current. This is important to do at the beginning of your swim in relatively shallow water because you want to estimate the best heading for your desired course. It might even warn you to exit the water or shorten your intended swim due to the conditions. You should plan to periodically check your drift due to currents throughout a swim.

<u>*Flat vs. Chop*</u>: The swimming techniques learned in a pool are tailored to flat water that is at least a meter deep—it's like you're *skating on* a surface. However, the sea can be choppy—you wish to *slice through* the water. **Be prepared to adjust your style when you're in open water.** These adjustments may occur minute by minute and hour to hour.

With sea chop you may need longer glides than in the pool. Imagine extending your hand forward through the water as if you wanted to push a needle horizontally through the chop, delaying the start of your pull from front to back. That momentary delay is called the glide—which can last for a full second—where your entire body becomes a needle, oriented horizontally in the water, with your head facing downward. A horizontal orientation can be perceived when the swimmer feels turbulent water motion around their buttocks, indicating the lower half of the body is near the surface instead of below. This gliding needle technique is also needed when swimming out through breaking waves. Instead of swimming up and over a wave, the correct technique is to shallow dive like a duck under and through the wave. (More powerful waves require a deeper dive forward.) You do *not* follow the surface.

For other situations and goals, you might revert to a shorter, quicker arm stroke. For example, the gliding needle stroke does not easily allow sighting forward. I've seen swimmers with wonderful glides swim in a wide arc and literally collide with an anchored boat as if they were blind. When the swimmer needs to sight forward, even if the water is choppy, the gliding needle technique may not be possible or beneficial.

Two more stroke adjustments pertain to the *recovery* (when the hand travels above the water) and the *pull* (when the hand is below the water). For the freestyle stroke in flat water, the wrists stay lower than the elbows (the wrists enter the water before the elbows do) and the swimmer chooses exactly where their hands will enter the water in front of them. This will not work well if choppy sea water is hitting the swimmer's wrist as it is moving forward above the water surface. The collision of a wave with the hand can injure a swimmer, particularly by straining the shoulder with the abrupt deceleration. The swimmer may have to raise their wrists more, possibly higher than the elbow, with a stroke that looks more like a windmill. If the wind is to your back, then a windmill-like arm recovery can accelerate your pace due to leeway. But, if you have a strong headwind, the arms should stay as low and streamlined as possible to minimize leeway.

At the same time, choppy water can jostle a swimmer from side-to-side. To stabilize this motion, the underwater pull may be wider, directed away from the side of the body, compared to a pool pull. I recall feeling horrified with my stroke when I was holding a selfie-stick in front of me in one hand, and swimming freestyle with the other hand. Above the water my stroke looked like a windmill, and below the water my hand pulled to the side. Yet, this was the correct stroke for that situation: everything I was doing compensated for the unbalanced one-handed swimming in open water.

I would also recommend slowing your stroke rhythm—less could be more. I usually find that hand/wave collisions happen (and hurt most) when I am swimming vigorously. When you are hit with chop, the natural response is to fight back, like a boxer, with a stronger, faster stroke. This can make things worse, injuring your arms and depleting your strength. Instead, approach the problem more harmoniously. Slow down the stroke with longer glides and by using a strong pull when your hand is below the water. You may feel like you are moving at a slower pace, yet you are avoiding injury and maintaining a sustainable speed.

With all the problems that may occur up front with the stroke, the steadiness and persistence of your kick is ever more important in a choppy sea. No matter what is happening up front, keep kicking!

Mindless vs. Mindful: People who do NOT like lap swimming in a pool will often remark that going back-and-forth repeatedly while staring at the pool floor is extremely boring. Admittedly, the safe and controlled pool environment allows the swimmer to become relatively mindless and focus attention on performance, or just daydream the entire time. Open water swimming, on the other hand, requires an engaged, alert, calculating, and forward-looking mindset that concerns performance AND attention to a complex and dynamic environment. One must plan ahead constantly, make decisions, remember a starting location, evaluate a path, sense the relative positions of vessels and other swimmers, monitor one's own physical fitness, and keep track of everything that is experienced over time. In a pool, the stakes are low if you stop to rest when you are tired and then decide to continue for another 400 m. In open water, this is a much more important question. If you start another 400 m without thinking and suffer a cramp after 150 m, the open water swim is not going to be as forgiving as a pool swim where you can simply stop and leave the water. In other words, do *not* approach an open water swim with the same mental state of a pool workout.

Unnatural vs. Natural: In the coastal water swims described here, you are a living creature exploring an environmental niche with other living creatures, and all are subject to the rules of natural selection—e.g., survival of the fittest. You will be leaving behind the human world and entering the wild. This very fact—experiencing a natural ecosystem— is the profound appeal of the swims that I will be sharing. However, the implicit risks are that the natural marine environment can be a danger to you. By comparison, pool swimming is a completely unnatural environment, with built-in layers of safety.

Just as the natural world can be a threat to humans, so too humans can be a threat to nature. If you leave behind plastic litter around a pool, someone is most likely going to clean it up. If you do the same on the beach, the wind can blow the plastic into the water and cause the death of marine life. Some of my swims are in pristine environments and your presence on the beach and in the water will have an impact. This impact is unavoidable but can and must be minimized to the best of your abilities.

Alone vs. Group: Swimming in a pool—even if there are other people in it—is quite often a solitary activity. For open water swimming, each and every swim should involve communication with other people. Even if you are swimming alone, a basic safety precaution is to tell someone what you are planning to do, even if it is just a phone conversation with a friend somewhere else. And if there's a lifeguard present, you should let them know as well.

Ideally, you will be swimming with at least one other person. Therefore, your swim group should discuss swim protocols, such as who will lead and how often or where everyone will stop to regroup, rest, assess everyone's health status, and make navigation decisions for the next segment of the swim. Simple protocols for assessing health could be a hand gesture (e.g., a thumbs-up from each swimmer) or, better yet, a hand gesture accompanied by a verbal statement such as, "I'm OK." A lot can be learned from how the verbal statement is spoken. Exhausted or otherwise physically challenged swimmers may not be able to speak, or the way they speak will reveal that they are having a problem.

Aquatics vs. Seamanship: In my opinion, the various pool and open water competitions are *aquatic* sports. However, unsupervised, open water swims (the term "wild swim" is sometimes used), even though they resemble an aquatic sport, should be considered something more akin to *seamanship*. On land, aquatic sports are like track and field, whereas open water swims are like mountaineering. In aquatic swims, the rules are codified by the sport. In coastal water swims, the rules are those of survival in nature. In the former you are one of many swimmers. In the latter, you are sea life, or an unmotorized small vessel among other vessels operating near you. In aquatics, someone else is deciding your next action. In seamanship, you are responsible for decisions. That means you need to have competence in navigation, weather forecasts, boat traffic patterns, and even marine biology or First Aid. In many ways, open water swimming shares more with scuba diving or kayaking than with competitive swimming.

Pre-Swim Checklist:

Daily research and planning: The most important daily activity is to check online for the wind forecasts and current conditions, such as:

www.windfinder.com
www.emy.gr/en (the Greek national weather service)
www.meteo.gr/sailingmaps-en.cfm (sailing maps)
www.meteo.gr/beaches-home.cfm (beach conditions)
www.vesselfinder.com (boat locations and tracks)

Before your swim, you can review the maps that I provide and interactively with online maps or apps such as Google Earth. A wealth of additional information about beaches can be found at www.cretanbeaches.com. Various Crete tourism apps also exist in the Google Play (Android) and Apple (iOS) stores. While studying maps or viewing the local geography, scan for possible water exit beaches along your planned course in case you need rest or have an emergency.

Assess local conditions: Once arriving at the beach, the wind strength and direction should be determined, the water conditions evaluated, and the boat traffic studied. The warning flags and locations of lifeguards should be noted. You will then be deciding which course would be safest, with the possibility that a different day or place would be a safer choice. If there are breaking waves, extra time and caution are needed to judge the safety of water entry and the potential for rip currents. If you notice a rip current, mentally mark its location relative to fixed landmarks. Note the timing of wave sets hitting the beach: you will probably find an alternating series of large and powerful waves (*set*) followed by a group of smaller and weaker waves (*lull*). If you decide that you can swim safely, time your water entry to coincide with the weaker waves. The same principle applies for timing your water exit.

Avoid dehydration: A common problem with travel is dehydration. The first day after arriving in Crete you may not be at the top of your game due to dehydration. And if you are arriving from a place that is not as sunny and warm as Crete, it may take a day or two to adapt to the Cretan summer environment. Be mindful of the fact that you have just taken a physically stressful strip and drink plenty of water. Remember too that if you get sunburned, you may become more susceptible to heat-related health problems.

Salt water adaptation: As noted earlier, the saltiness of the water may trigger physically taxing coughing or other totally unexpected difficulties. Spend some time appreciating the buoyancy of the water, noting how much easier it is to float on your back compared to a swimming pool. Notice that you can steadily reduce your effort and continue to float. This awareness will be important to recall if you later find yourself panicking.

Cold shock adaptation: Some people have medical difficulties when they rapidly transition from warmer to colder environments. These temperatures are relative. When you are baking in the sun on the beach, even sea water that is considered warm can give you a cold shock. The gasp reflex—an immediate and involuntary breath, also known as the mammalian diving reflex—could occur when your face suddenly encounters cool water. You could aspirate salt water and drown. My advice is to be mindful of your sensitivity to cold shock when you first arrive on Crete. Your first few encounters with the water should be gradual: walk in slowly at your own pace as opposed to running or diving in. Try dipping your hands into the water first and then splashing it on your face. Contemplate how the cooler water may be affecting your heart rate, breathing, balance, vision, hearing, thinking, and speech. Irregular heartbeats, gasping, disorientation, tunnel vision, loss of hearing, and difficulty speaking are signs of physical distress.

Warm-up and stretching: If you know thyself, you will have a good idea of how much warm-up and stretching you might need for a particular swim. My routine varies depending on the length of my intended swim and the body areas where I may be feeling particularly tight. This routine may be repeated after the swim and some stretches are possible during the swim.

A typical swimmer's warm-up includes circular arm motions (forward and backward circles, varying the diameter from tiny to large) and swinging the arms across the torso. Some swimmers entering cold water will warm up more vigorously to raise their body temperature before taking the plunge.

The warm-up is followed by stretching, particularly the forearms, arms, and shoulders. Hold a stretch for more than 10 seconds and be mindful of relaxing and improving the stretch with each breath exhalation. A uniquely "swimmer's stretch" is to raise one hand holding the corner of a towel above and behind your head, then pull the towel downward using your free hand behind your back. Or hold the towel at each end in front of you—arms straight and wide—and then rotate your arms up above your head and behind your back. One of my favorites is pressing one hand firmly against the side of my head above the ear for 10 seconds, while the other hand presses the base of the neck on the other side, and then switching. This loosens up tense neck muscles and I repeat it during breaks in the water—my swim technique noticeably improves afterwards. I also try leg stretches and a general loosening up around the waist. Perhaps the best all-around stretch for me is the [downward dog](#) from yoga, which can be modified by grasping a raised object in front of you (e.g., a beach umbrella post or a chair).

Easy swims first: Try swimming a bit at a leisurely pace, parallel to the shore, and possibly in shallow water, simply to test yourself, your gear, and water conditions such as temperature and visibility. There will be plenty of time to challenge yourself later.

Night swims: Night swims are meant to be novel, fun experiences closer to shore and shorter in duration than day swims. Always try your intended night swim during the day, paying particular attention to any difficulties in entering and exiting the water, and carefully noting the landmarks needed to return to the beach from the swimmer's perspective. Staying warm is a concern, so plan to have warm, dry clothing. And I'd recommend bringing two beach towels. One towel will inevitably get wet and never dry out until the next day, which means your second towel will be a handy backup. You will also need enough light to do things on the beach. In the past I've used my mobile phone light but found it to be clumsy to use in the dark with wet and sandy hands. I much prefer a small LED flashlight with a lantern mode. They can be found at the small shops near beaches in case you forget to bring one from home.

Group pre-swim briefing: Before entering the water, swimmers should discuss the weather conditions, what they hope to achieve, and what they want to avoid during the swim. As mentioned earlier, protocols can be reviewed, such as the frequency and duration of rest breaks, perhaps agreeing to stop if the group is spread out by more than 50 m. Discuss who will be the leader. Disclose and review health issues and supplies. Also, the group could agree on using certain hand signals given that swimmers may spread out in the water over time. **Waving one arm widely over the head is an emergency distress call.** Holding one hand straight up (as if in a school classroom) could be taken as a non-urgent request for someone to approach. A thumbs-up gesture could be used to indicate that a message was understood or that the swimmer is OK. When a swimmer finds something interesting underwater, they could raise one hand in front of them and point a finger downward toward the water. Another possible gesture is when the group leader stops and raises a clenched fist over their head, then that means everyone should stop and/or swim towards the leader. A leader could also use a whistle to communicate.

Καλή βουτιά! (ka-LEE vou-TIA or Happy Swimming!)

I hope that this chapter offered useful insights into swimming preparation and safety not only for excursions around Crete, but also for open water swims anywhere on our beautiful blue planet. In the following chapters you will be experiencing wonderful swims all around the island. I will now happily send the readers off to their new swimming adventures with a Cretan lyrical poem called a mantinada (morning song):

Ήθελα μόνο μια στιγμή	I just wanted for a moment
τσι θάλασσας να μοιάσω,	to resemble the vast sea,
για να μπορέσω ολόκληρη	encircling Crete with my arms
την Κρήτη ν' αγκαλιάσω.	and hugging her close to me.

3

North Coast of Crete

THE NORTH COAST IS MORE DEVELOPED AND LESS PRISTINE than the south coast of Crete. The 95,000 square kilometers of water between Crete's northern coastline and the [Cyclades islands](#) (e.g., Santorini and Milos) is called the [Cretan Sea](#) (which is a portion of the Aegean Sea), and this is where you will be swimming. With the prevailing northwesterly winds, many beaches facing north will likely have rough water. Most of the swims I will be recommending are partially protected because the beaches face northeast or east, and in some cases south. Nevertheless, if the weather forecasts are for high winds on some days and low wind on other days, it makes sense to plan the north coast swims for the low wind days.

The 12 swim locations I've chosen on the north coast are presented from west to east rather than ranking them based on their characteristics or my personal favorites. Consider also that your day-to-day itinerary can have an axis of exploration that is north–south rather than east–west. In other words, if you are staying on the western half of the island, say Chania on the north coast, then the closest north coast swims are around Chania (Balos **#1** and Marathi **#2**). But instead of continuing farther east the next day to try the swims near Rethymno or Heraklion, one could stay on the western part of the island and enjoy the swims on the south coast (Sfakia **#20** and Elafonisi **#21**), which would be day trips from

Chania. Later you could shift over to the Rethymno and Heraklion areas and do the swims on both the north and south coasts for the middle and eastern parts of the island.

#1 Balos-Gramvousa

The northwest tip of Crete hosts the world-class Balos Beach (35°35'02.0"N 23°35'25.7"E) with jaw-dropping views, turquoise waters, white and pink sand, and a wild, mountainous environment that will enthrall nature lovers. A shallow lagoon lies south of the beach and a remarkable Venetian fortress towers on an island to the north called Gramvousa. My top-level advice is to arrive by car and stay for an unforgettable sunset that surpasses even the beauty of Santorini's famous caldera sunset.

There are two main options for traveling to Balos. The first requires boarding a ferry from the port of Kissamos in the morning or looking for organized tours from hotels and vendors. The advantage of the ferry services is that they may stop at the island of Gramvousa where you can climb up to its Venetian fortress with its spectacular views. One can also swim at Gramvousa Beach and explore the 1968 shipwreck of the *Dimitrios P*. (35°36'24.6"N 23°34'53.9"E). Afterwards the ferry might take you to Balos Beach. The disadvantage is that the ferry does not allow you to stay until sunset. On the other hand, a ferry allows you to enjoy the beaches of Gramvousa and Balos without climbing any steps.

The second option is to drive 8 km on a dirt road to a parking area high (140 m) above Balos Beach, and then descend carefully on foot to sea level along a path with steps. The advantages of this approach are stopping at the lookout points to marvel at the lagoon from high above when you arrive during the day, and then returning to the lookout points after the beach closes at 8 pm and lingering to watch a stunning sunset. The disadvantages are the dirt-road driving (most rental cars seem to survive), the strenuous climb for 1.1 km back up to the parking area at the end of the day, and not seeing Gramvousa unless you swim across. One can stay at Balos Beach up until the point when a guard starts blowing a whistle for visitors to leave.

There are many possibilities for swims at Balos Beach that will depend on how you arrive in the area, what you want to see, how far you want to swim, and the strength and direction of the wind. The shortest swims are in shallow water north of Balos Beach as well as in the deep-water bay to the southwest. The map shows a 1.6-km route on the southwest side where you will experience complete isolation from people and boats. It is important to stop and gauge the wind and current which will typically be pushing you south. I did not find any caves along this stretch of coastline but floating in the small bays protected from the northwesterlies was a pleasure.

If you wish to swim between Gramvousa and Balos, you should first study the boat traffic (warning triangles on the map) when you arrive to evaluate the safety of the crossing. Check www.vesselfinder.com too. A **large swim buoy is needed** to make yourself visible to the numerous boats and ferries. It may be safest to **swim early in the morning** before the tour boats arrive around 10:30 am. Stop your swim often to assess the traffic. If boats are approaching, lift your buoy above the water to become more visible. I would only cross in very light wind and nearly flat conditions. Given all these requirements, the crossing is not guaranteed and swimming along the coastlines should be your default plan.

The map shows an isolated starting beach (35°35'38.2"N 23°35'35.7"E) that is reached after swimming or walking 1.1 km north of Balos Beach along the east side of the bay. The walk is over rocks near the shoreline, and I would wear sturdy shoes. The swim from this starting beach across to Gramvousa Beach is roughly 2 km and an islet serves as a resting spot and for sighting the course. The islet lies 800 m along a northwest diagonal route from the starting beach. The swimmer needs to check for oncoming vessels, enter the water when none are approaching, and swim to it quickly. The crossing between the islet and Gramvousa Beach with its shipwreck is 1.2 km and again requires extreme caution. If you plan to explore the Venetian fortress, bring light footwear, money, and clothing in your swim buoy. Drinking water may not be available at Gramvousa.

If you arrive in Gramvousa by ferry, you could explore the Venetian fortress first, and then swim to Balos Beach using the course described above. A northwesterly wind would be to your back and help in your pace. At Balos Beach, you would meet the same ferry again for the return trip to Kissamos. The swim is therefore one-way only. Your shoes and clothes could be left on the ferry the entire time, while your valuables could be kept in a swim buoy.

#2 Marathi Island

Chania is the westernmost large city of Crete and perhaps the most attractive of the island, which also means that huge crowds visit its old harbor during the peak summer months. The Akrotiri Peninsula lies east of Chania and hosts the airport. Among its many beaches, the northernmost at Stavros is where the final dance scene of *Zorba the Greek* was filmed. The geography of its eastern coastline has several mini-fjords, including one named Seitan Limani (Stefanou Beach) that appears in many photographs and videos (see Chapter 5).

My recommended swim starts from the south-facing town of Marathi which is roughly 17 km from Chania or a 25-minute drive. Marathi has a small harbor with sandy beaches on either side to the east and west. All are viable water-entry points and I will choose the beach just east of the boat harbor (35°30'17.34"N 24°10'26.66"E) where it is a roughly 600-m swim over to a sandy beach (35°30'1.25"N 24°10'39.57"E) on the small (but not tiny) island called Palaiosouda. Circumnavigating the island adds 1,300 m. Thus, if you wish to simply go back-and-forth, this is a 1,200-m swim, but if you add the circumnavigation, you will roughly double the distance. Note that Marathi can become very crowded with beachgoers, particularly on Sundays, and the reason is the attraction of its family-friendly sandy and shallow water. You will find all the usual beach amenities and many tavernas as well.

One can also enter the water southwest of Marathi at Loutraki Beach (35°29'56.46"N 24°9'50.47"E), in which case the swim distance one-way due east to the island is 1,200 m. One could choose the 600-m swim from Marathi on the first day, see how it goes, and then attempt the 1,200-m approach from Loutraki on the second day. My main warning is that there tends to be a current coming from the northeast that will push the swimmer southwest, even on days with light winds. A swimmer will need to assess their drift vector (speed and direction) and adjust their heading to stay on course. Also note that the low profile of the island somehow makes it look closer than it really is.

Indeed, I found that circumnavigating the island clockwise is psychologically interesting. First, as you swim from Marathi towards its northern shoreline, everything seems safe because you can look back and see civilization. The water becomes shallow near the island, and you can walk up onto small beaches. In fact, you can explore much of the island barefoot and this adds greatly to the appeal of this swim.

But as you continue swimming eastward, with the island's coastline on your right, and then turn the corner to swim south, it seems like you are suddenly in the open ocean all by yourself. Indeed, you have ventured so far east, that you are now directly exposed to the wind and waves coming from the north. The water is deeper and darker, the rocky face of the island is steeper, and you may start feeling anxious about where you are swimming. This is a good time to practice calming your mind and anchoring your thoughts on the skills and professionalism involved in open water swimming.

I would recommend double-checking the map of the island before you start and refer to the section on sighting illusions earlier in the book. You may think you have almost finished swimming around it, but in reality you may have only reached the half-way point. Recall that crossing over to the island is 600 m, but then you have another 1,300 m to circumnavigate it. If you keep this in mind, you are less likely to feel surprise and anxiety that you are not finishing the circumnavigation as soon as you thought you would. Notice that the island has a rectangular shape so that as you swim east and make your first right turn to go south, you are still swimming away from Marathi. This is not the "back" of the island quite yet. You need to continue and make another right turn to head west—that is when you are on the back of the island (from the perspective of your starting point at Marathi).

I would not recommend circumnavigating the island if the first 600-m segment has exhausted you. Even on very light wind days, I have felt the current pushing me towards the southwest, and on windier days you will need to check your drift more often. If you examine the anchored sailboats in my photo from Marathi's beach, which was taken on a light wind day, their bows are pointing to the left. That is the eastward direction and shows where the current is coming from. Therefore, the swimmer will be pushed to the right, or westward.

#3 Kamari Gastroswim

My friend Petros Parthenis founded WeSwim.gr in Athens and he coined the term "gastroswim" for his unique swimming excursions that include fine local dining and wine-tasting. The food in Crete is generally excellent so that every place you visit will seem like a gastroswim. However, one village that is rather special for dining in Crete is Argyroupolis ([35°17'11.6"N 24°19'55.6"E](#)) with its "waterfall tavernas." Here you can eat outdoors under the abundant trees and greenery with natural spring water coursing through the tavernas in small waterfalls and pools. My favorite dish is lamb "[antikristo](#)" which means "opposite the fire." Instead of placing meat over a fire and cooking it rapidly, it is hung around the fire and cooked slowly. If you are a connoisseur of both barbecues and waterfalls, you will love this place!

My suggested swim spot for this gastroswim is roughly 10 km west of Rethymno where we find the inland village of Gerani and Kamari Beach on the coast. Note that there is a "Gerani Beach" west of Chania which might incorrectly show up in your web searches. Kamari Beach is located just 20 minutes west of Spilies Beach (swim #4) and you could swim at both locations easily in a day. The drive from Kamari to Argyroupolis is 16 km or roughly 20 minutes. Kamari has a church on the seashore and beaches both east and west of the church. The water will be rough on days with substantial northwesterlies; the western beach will be the most protected.

Swimming 200 m to the left of the westernmost beach (35°21'38.32"N 24°24'24.73"E), we find a fairly large sea cave (West Cave), which may be hard to see at first because of a large rock blocking a direct view of the entrance. It has a shallow sandy bottom, and you can rest by standing on it. Immediately to the right of the easternmost beach (35°21'36.74"N 24°24'33.48"E), the rock formation resembles Swiss cheese, with openings for the swimmer to enter from the sea and small holes that bring in light from above. Swimmers can choose which side to start with and then swim 300 m across to the other side. For a longer route, one can swim 1 km northeastward along the shoreline, exploring all the nooks and crannies along the way.

#4 Spilies Tunnel and Sea Arch

The 30-m long tunnel and 30-m high arch that you will find near Spilies Beach (35°24'37.5"N 24°38'18.1"E) are genuinely rare geological features for the coastline of Crete, and perhaps the entire Mediterranean. The most famous sea arch in the Mediterranean, the Azure Window on the Maltese island of Goza, collapsed in 2017. Most other sea arches are difficult to reach, often requiring a paid boat excursion. Three examples are Tripiti on the southern tip of Gavdos (south of Crete), Kleftiko on the southwest coast of Milos (north of Crete), and the Blue Caves on the northeast coast of Zakynthos (in the Ionian Sea). Yet, here at Spilies, a short drive off the motorway, we find a natural sea arch comparable in size to the Azure Window.

Notice that the map shows a dotted line for the course departing Spilies Beach to the right and it crosses land twice. This does NOT mean you are leaving the water for a short hike. Instead, these are the points where you are swimming UNDERNEATH rock. The first passage is the tunnel and the second is the arch. There are also several caves to swim into.

The tunnel is immediately to the right (east) of Spilies Beach. Roughly 200 m to the left you will find a large cave and two more after that if you swim an additional 300 m. The beach itself also has cave-like features which provide cave-shade during the day. One might also see people cliff diving along the rocks to the left and right. A beach larger than Spilies that may be easier to find is called Geropotamos Beach (35°24'49.4"N 24°38'43.2"E). The arch is an equidistant swim from both beaches (350 m). Both beaches have the usual amenities of beach umbrellas and chairs for rent, as well as food and water. Swimming between Spilies and Geropotamos beach is roughly 700 m, and one passes through both the arch and the tunnel along the way.

However, I recommend swimming at these locations only if the water is fairly flat. Both beaches face north-northwest and they are directly exposed to wind and waves. The swim to the arch will be very rough and I have heard reports of strong currents. The swim through the tunnel could be very dangerous. When you look at wind forecasts, you should plan this swim for days when the northwesterlies are below four Beaufort (or if the forecast is for southerlies).

Note that the motorway exits for the narrow roads to Spilies beach are marked by very small signs which may simply say "Beach." I would suggest driving slowly on the right so that you do not miss the turnoffs. Finally, I would highly recommend watching the sunset while floating in the water near the arch. If the wind is calm and the water is relatively flat, this will be a peaceful and visually unforgettable experience.

#5 Bali (the one in Crete)

A 30-minute drive east of Rethymno or 50 minutes west of Heraklion we find the bay and coastal village of Bali, which means "honey" in Turkish and has no relation to the famous Indonesian island. Bali is sweet for swimmers given that the cape offers protection from the northwesterlies. Since the beaches can be overcrowded and there are watersport boats using the southern portion of the bay, I would recommend swims from the northernmost beach along the west side of the bay called Karavostasis (35°25'00.8"N 24°47'07.0"E), where the "Evita" taverna and rooms are located. Here you will park above the sandy beach and walk down to it, where you will find all the usual amenities. Since the beach is only 50-m wide, it can feel just as crowded as all the other beaches in Bali. Short swims would involve hugging the coastline for 150 m or more to the left and to the right.

For a longer workout, I enjoy swimming southeast 935 m across the bay to the opposite side (35°24'40.3"N 24°47'34.6"E). Admittedly this is a simple swim and with the deep waters there is not much to see, which is why I would call it a "workout swim." As you travel farther away from the beach and the open sea starts hitting you, make sure to stop and evaluate whether or not you think it is safe for you to continue all the way to the other side. Remember, it will be harder to swim back against the weather.

#6 The Green Coast – Agia Pelagia

The coastline becomes mountainous just west of Heraklion with a characteristic green rock, and thus I call it Crete's "Green Coast." The ancient Minoans used this beautiful rock to pave their streets and palaces. The famed British archaeologist Sir Arthur Evans took stones from this region to restore parts of ancient Knossos.

The area is also known as Agia Pelagia (Saint Pelagia), which is the name of the largest beach and fishing village. A major reason the Green Coast is known to local swimmers is that the capes and peninsulas protect much (but not all) of the coastline from strong northwesterlies that create rough conditions on many of the other beaches along the entire northern coast of the island. Locals also warn of currents, and I recommend that swimmers stay relatively near the coastline from bay to bay.

The bay in front of Agia Pelagia is where I had a one-of-a-kind swimming experience when I was a kid. Swimming straight out some 200 m I thought I saw the giant head of an ancient statue lying on the seafloor. I left the spot to get my cousins but was unable to return to the same place to show them the statue. I came to believe that it must have been a plain old rock that looked like a head—how is it possible that no one else noticed a 4,000-year-old marble head lying in relatively shallow water?

Forty years later I was having a nice lunch at Socrates Taverna on the beachfront of Agia Pelagia. I asked the owner, Manos Kaloyerakis—nicknamed "the Monk," who is also a local mountain bike expert with advice on equipment and trails—if he had seen an ancient marble head when he swam there as a kid.

Yes, he had! Agia Pelagia is the site of the ancient city of Apollonia, and the head was subsequently removed from the sea by archaeologists. The moral of the story: if the reader is swimming along and sees something on the seafloor that looks like a 4,000-year-old marble head, it might actually be a 4,000-year-old marble head.

The five main beaches of the Green Coast from southeast to northwest are Mades, Ligaria, Agia Pelagia, Psaromoura, and Mononaftis. Some maps may show a beach called Kladissos south of Psaromoura, but access to the beach is made difficult by a walled and guarded hotel built on Cape Souda. **Greek law designates all natural beaches freely open to the public**, so a swimmer could request entrance at the hotel gate to walk to the beach.

My first insider's recommended swim starts from the Peninsula Resort which always keeps a small, unguarded gate open for visitors. The water entry point is a cement platform (35°24'51.1"N 25°01'12.1"E) built on the south side of the hotel adjacent to Psaromoura Beach. Psaromoura is a sandy/pebbly beach and easier to find, but local Cretans come to Peninsula (particularly on Sundays) because people can dive right into the few meter deep waters from the platform and encounter excellent underwater visibility. Swimmers climb back up to the platform using a ladder, and they can rent the hotel's sunbeds and umbrellas, plus eat and drink at the cantina located at the back of the platform.

To reach either Peninsula or Psaromoura, one drives to the smaller Eva Mare Hotel where the road dead-ends at a small dirt parking area overlooking the sea. One may have to make a U-turn and find parking a bit farther back along the road. From this small parking area, you can walk a path to the right (as you face the sea) and descend towards Psaromoura, or walk a bit uphill to the left, go up cement stairs, and pass through a small gate into the Peninsula Resort. After the gate, the rest of your path is downhill towards the platform. Both Psaromoura and Peninsula require significant downhill and uphill walking. One difference is that Psaromoura has a freshwater shower while the Peninsula platform does not.

My recommended swim is to dive from the Peninsula cement platform and swim south straight across to the cliffs on the other side (35°24'35.2"N 25°01'15.2"E)—this is the northern coastline of Cape Souda which has a hotel on top of it. The cliffs are steep, and you will see some stairs hugging the rock from the sea up to the hotel. Given the swim distance of 475 m, it is handy for pool swimmers to compare their swim time here with one of their 500-m pool workouts. The northwesterlies will push you along and improve your time as you swim to Cape Souda, and then you will have to battle the oncoming weather as you return to Peninsula. Instead of struggling against the oncoming chop, you can return by hugging the coast to the left and visit the beaches of Kladissos and Psaromoura. Keep an eye out above the surface not only for watercraft, but also for signs of monk seals and dolphins that have occasionally been spotted here.

For a longer swim (an additional 400 m), continue south by going around Cape Souda and hugging the coast to the right as you approach the beach of Agia Pelagia. The picturesque area to the right (the south side of Cape Souda) has green waters, green rocks, and small coves named Fylakes (Prisons) because the occupying Turks had used them as prisons. This is also the area of the Apollonia archaeological site. You will find larger crowds and more boats in the bay of Agia Pelagia, which is why many swimmers prefer the relative peace and quiet of swimming only in the zone between Peninsula and Cape Souda.

My second recommended swim has an entry point at Mades Beach (35°24'00.7"N 25°02'01.9"E) which is the southeasternmost beach of the Green Coast. From this sandy beach, you will see two islets to the left. If you swim straight out, circumnavigate the islets, and return to the beach, that will be a 900-m swim. If the northwesterlies are light, one can swim a longer route by hugging the coastline to the right (east) for 800 m and exploring a cave (35°24'03.3"N 25°02'32.9"E) at the neck of the Tripiti Peninsula. The cave is visible from a distance, appearing elevated above a beach that has small, rounded rocks.

CRETE SWIM

Amazingly, once you ascend into the cave, you discover that it drops down into another beach cave on the opposite side. Thus, the peninsula has a "hole" in it. Though I have explored the beach and cave barefoot, I would recommend bringing along some light slippers in a swim buoy to minimize the discomfort of walking on the rocks.

The Green Coast has many other options for beach entries and swim courses. For example, one could enter the water at the northwesternmost beach called Mononaftis and hug the coastline southward. Visiting every beach until reaching the "hole" (Tripiti) amounts to a 5.5-km swim.

#7 Paleokastro Caves

One of the closest beaches west of Heraklion is called Paleokastro (old castle) and there are sea caves 1 km and 2.2 km north of it. The long, rocky, steep coastline faces east but the water can be rough due to northerly winds. As you swim farther north, the coastline curves eastward and will offer increasing protection. Indeed, this area is where I once saw the space-age super-yacht of Russian billionaire Andrey Melnichenko, the largest sailing vessel in the world at 142 m long and sporting three high-tech masts shooting 90 m into the sky.

I am not fond of Paleokastro Beach itself (35°21'58.1"N 25°02'19.4"E) because the motorway bridge right above it is an eyesore next to the 12th century Venetian fort. For those with mobility challenges, one advantage of the beach is the relatively easy access from the car parking to the water, as well as the usual amenities of a freshwater shower, changing shed, and tavernas nearby.

The closest sea caves (35°22'30.1"N 25°02'15.9"E) lie 1 km north of the beach, featuring narrow passageways to swim through and explore. The cave located 1.2 km (35°23'05.6"N 25°02'24.2"E) farther north is interesting because it has two entrances that are hard to find and fun to discover. There is a south-facing entrance where you carefully exit the water to walk into the cave with its pebbly bottom. Inside the cave, you can re-enter the water and exit by swimming through a low and narrow tunnel facing east. The tunnel has just enough clearance around you for a very careful swim.

This double-entranced cave also provides me an opportunity to quiz you: If there is a tall cave opening facing south and a second opening that's a low and narrow tunnel facing east, which one do you choose to enter, and which do you exit? In this scenario, the wind and waves are coming from the north.

The correct answer is to enter from the southern opening and exit to the east. The guiding principle comes from one of my safety tips: *Always face the direction of danger.* If you swim into the east entrance, the waves are behind you and to your right. It will be difficult to foresee how the waves will jostle you around as you enter the cave and they can unexpectedly knock you against the hard rock. If you enter from the south, you are swimming *into* the direction of danger and the waves will be in front of you where you can see them, plus the land itself partially shields you from the waves. When you leave the cave through the tunnel facing east, then you are again swimming *into* the potentially hazardous oncoming waves. If a threatening wave is approaching, you have time to take a breath and dive down and forward, thus avoiding the rising water pushing you up into the tunnel ceiling. Nevertheless, if the waves in this hypothetical example are really that threatening, I would not recommend using the east tunnel at all.

#8 Knossos Final Approach

If you are seated on a plane making its final approach for landing at Heraklion's Nikos Kazantzakis International Airport (HER), then you probably just passed over this swim spot. The altitude is low enough that if you have sharp eyes, you may even see some swimmers out of the windows on the left side of the plane during the day. Likewise, as a swimmer you can look up and wave a warm welcome for the arriving passengers. If your two hobbies happen to be swimming and plane spotting, then this swim will make you very happy indeed.

However, if you arrive in Crete after 2025, the airport will have a new location 39 km southeast of Heraklion in the town of Kasteli. Thus, your swim will not include low-flying passenger aircraft. On the other hand, the significance of this swim's starting point at Amnisos Beach hasn't changed for thousands of years: It's the site of the [Amnisos archaeological](#) area and the ancient port for the extraordinary Minoan palace of Knossos. For centuries, this must have been "Knossos Final Approach" as ships from all over Greece, Egypt, and the rest of the Mediterranean arrived here to visit and trade with the Minoans. Indeed, [according to Homer](#), as Odysseus was sailing from Ithaca to Troy, strong winds forced him to anchor his ships at Amnisos:

> "There is a land called Crete, in the midst of the wine-dark sea, a fair, rich land, begirt with water, and therein are many men, past counting, and ninety cities. They have not all the same speech, but their tongues are mixed. There dwell Achaeans, there great-hearted native Cretans, there Cydonians, and Dorians of waving plumes, and goodly Pelasgians. Among their cities is the great city Cnosus, where Minos reigned when nine years old, he that held converse with great Zeus… There it was that I saw Odysseus and gave him gifts of entertainment; for the force of the wind had brought him too to Crete, as he was making for the land of Troy, and drove him out of his course past Malea. So he anchored his ships at **Amnisus**, where is the cave of Eilithyia, in a difficult harbor, and hardly did he escape the storm."

Long story short, people must have been swimming at Amnisos 5,000 years ago, maybe even the great Odysseus! One can still visit the cave of Eilithyia 2 km inland from the beach, though the cave entrance is blocked by an iron fence.

The Amnisos entry point ([35°19'56.7"N 25°12'23.9"E](#)) is in front of the restaurant and beach volleyball club called [News Cafe Beach](#) (a bar, cafe, and restaurant). The modern name for this area is Karteros, and you will be swimming in Karteros Bay. The first swim destination is an islet called Monocharako ([35°20'08.9"N 25°12'19.0"E](#)), a roughly northward swim of 400 m from Amnisos Beach. If you circumnavigate Monocharako (250 m), then the entire swim out-and-back is roughly 1050 m. Though the beach entry point begins with a plain sandy bottom, the area around the islet becomes shallower with rocks and sea life, making the trip worthwhile. News Cafe Beach has all the usual amenities such as showers, changing sheds, and toilets, as well as delicious snacks, coffees, food, and drinks. If it is too crowded or the music is not to your liking, you can easily walk a short distance to emptier parts of the beach to the east or west.

If you visit the Heraklion Archaeological Museum, you will find a famous Minoan wall fresco depicting white lilies on a red background that came from an ancient 10-room home at Amnisos, now called the "Villa of the Lilies." The ruins of this villa are located southwest of the parking lot of New Cafe Beach at the foot of a hill called Paleochora. On the northwest side of the hill, just 30 m from the shoreline, more ruins can be viewed which represent the ancient harbor of Knossos and a temple to Zeus.

In addition to beach volleyball, there's a water sports rental shack east of News Cafe Beach with jet skis, pedal boats, SUPs, etc. Your friends who do not want to swim to the island could accompany you on a pedal boat. You might also see a large buoy to the east of Monocharako—this marks a jet ski boundary and it should not be approached (triangle on the map). Note that parking is difficult here (and everywhere) on Sundays, particularly if the weather is calm and hot.

These beaches are not well-protected from the north and northwesterly winds, as Homer wrote, and I would not recommend the swim if Heraklion Airport is reporting greater than 14 knots (>26 km/h or 4 Beaufort). However, the breaking waves on windy days can be fun for body surfing, but with higher winds they can be dangerous. A lifeguard once asked me to stop body surfing just because other people were seeing me, entering the water to do the same, but they were not experienced in dealing with the waves and were thus risking their lives. I was happy to comply.

Having said that, windy conditions can be valuable as practice for good swimmers to learn how to dive and swim through a breaking wave rather than going up and over it. Remember to keep your freestyle kick strong and your body sleek as you dive into, under, and through the waves (often called a duck dive). You can swim out 100 m and then come back, getting a feel for gliding your body forward with the swells, and stroking and kicking hard after the swell passes and the water pushes you back. You should also practice resting by floating in the water and always facing the direction of the oncoming waves. Though this sounds like a simple task, open water swimmers should automatically turn their heads to face oncoming waves, and this requires repeated practice. A more difficult task to practice is swimming into the waves and sighting forward continuously so you can know when to dive through a wave. It is too dangerous to swim with the head facing down as if in a swimming pool and have a breaking wave hit you without expecting it.

Furthermore, with its sandy bottom and lights from the News Cafe Beach, this area is nice for a night swim on calm evenings. You will likely see the sparkles of a few bioluminescent plankton as you dive in. The lights from the cafe will keep you oriented, though the light pollution of Crete's north coast interferes with viewing the stars. Before it gets dark, many people will linger on the beach to watch the peaceful sunset, and you can even order food and drinks that will be brought to your beach chairs.

If the sea is very calm, I can recommend a second swim eastward to Boufos Cave ([35°20'05.0"N 25°13'22.1"E](#)), one of the largest in Crete in terms of both height and depth. A wide hole in the ceiling lets in plenty of sunlight and birds will fly in and out from all directions. One can shorten the swim to 1 km by first walking along the sandy shoreline from Amnisos to the eastern end of the beach. As you swim to the cave, stop to make sure that sea current is not so strong that returning to Amnisos will exceed your abilities.

To summarize, the swim to Monocharako is fairly short and will help you acclimatize to the Cretan waters. On days with breaking waves and chop beyond the surf zone, you will be able to practice your technique with more difficult conditions. This is a lifeguarded beach as well, and there are other swimmers going back and forth. If the sea is calm, the 2 km roundtrip swim to Boufos Cave is highly recommended. The sunsets are beautiful and a night swim can also be enjoyable. Finally, the shallow area near the islet has plenty of sea life, and it's impressive to watch large planes flying low right in front of you, or at least imagining the great Odysseus piloting his boats into the bay.

#9 Hersonissos Coves

Travelling eastward from Heraklion, the coast is generally north-facing for 18 km, and then it curves southward at Cape Sarandaris, offering a protected area for swimming between the Knossos Royal and Creta Maris hotels in the coastal village of Hersonissos. Note that the CretAquarium is a 15-minute drive (11 km) to the west of this location. Hersonissos is one of the more touristy/party areas of Crete, but this east-facing coastline between the two hotels has a series of sandy coves which are very pleasant. However, they generally do not have freshwater showers or changing rooms.

The first swim starts from the southernmost coves ([35°19'35.6"N 25°23'13.5"E](#)) which border the north side of the Creta Maris hotel. I like how these coves (nicknamed "limanakia") have sand with minuscule shells that you can spend hours sifting through. This type of sand always strikes me as "perfect" because it does not get too hot, nor does it easily stick to your skin and make a huge mess later in your car or room. The swim course is 410 m northeastward to a lonely rock in the middle of the water ([35°19'45.2"N 25°23'25.1"E](#)). As you approach it, the area becomes shallower and has interesting coral to swim over. The port of Hersonissos has several resident loggerhead sea turtles (*Caretta caretta*), and you may encounter these graceful creatures on your journey. During the high season, the recreational boat traffic might be disconcerting. **A swim buoy is recommended.** Most vessels will pass on the outside of the rock but sometimes they pass on the inside (between the rock and the beach) ...so stay alert!

The second swim begins from the northernmost cove ([35°20'06.8"N 25°23'03.4"E](#)) and the course is northeast 410 m to an islet ([35°20'15.9"N 25°23'16.1"E](#)) off the tip of Cape Sarandaris. This is probably the most protected swim I can think of on the north coast of Crete since the coastline is jutting out eastward, blocking the weather from the north. It is here that I will occasionally challenge myself by swimming butterfly in the flat water. Given the excellent weather protection provided by Cape Sarandaris, multiple tour boat businesses will anchor their vessels near here during the high season.

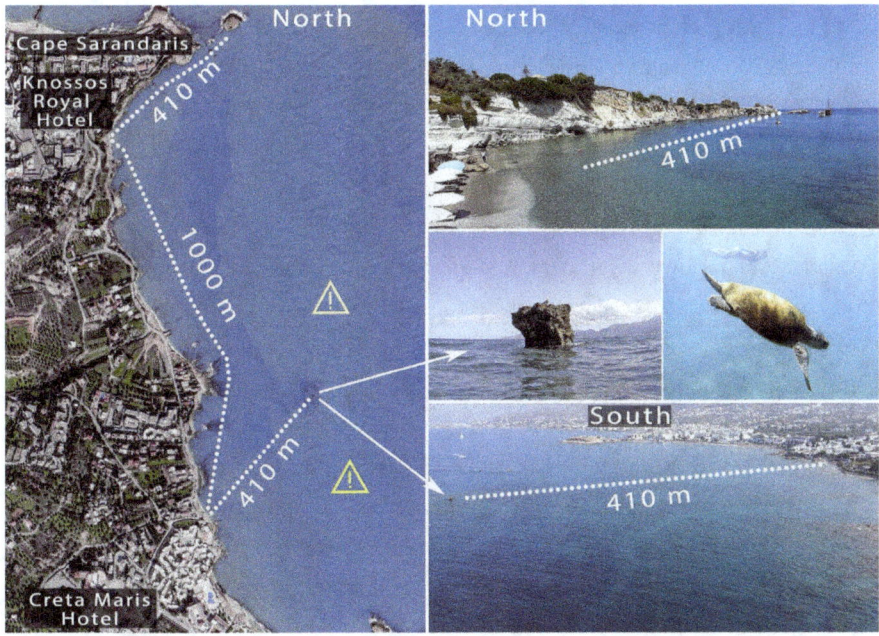

For a third swim, one can enter the water at the southernmost cove and instead of heading northeast to the rock, swim north 1 km to the northernmost cove, rest in the calm waters, and swim back south again to the starting point, thus providing a 2 km total swim. Of course, swimmers can begin and finish at the northern cove if they wish. Whatever the case, hugging the coastline is the safest option since you will avoid boat traffic.

#10 Artemisia's Swim – Plaka to Spinalonga

This swim from the town of Plaka to the Venetian fortress of Spinalonga (also known as the island of Kalydon) qualifies as an "insider's swim" given that my mother's side of the family came from the town of Plaka, and my grandmother Artemisia (1902–1952)—a talented swimmer in her own right—swam this course over a century ago.

Sometimes I wonder if she was drawn to the sea because of another Artemisia who lived 2,500 years ago and became the most famous and accomplished female naval commander in history. Allied with Xerxes I, she wowed everyone with her brilliance and valor in the Battle of Salamis between the Persians and the Greeks. My grandmother Artemisia Drettakis (née Papastefanakis) is now buried at a small church (Agia Marina) a stone's throw from Plaka's shoreline along with my great grandfather Panayiotis Papastefanakis, from the nearby village of Louma, and great grandmother Maria (née Grammatikakis), from the nearby village of Fourni. I think Artemisia would be delighted to know that her grandson and great grandchildren are continuing the family tradition—she might say that the sea water flows in our veins. (Το θαλασσινό νερό ρέει στις φλέβες μας.)

Studying a map of Crete, one notices that the beaches both north and south of Agios Nikolaos are protected from the prevailing westerlies and north westerlies. Indeed, a seaplane called the Short S. 17 Kent Flying Boat used to land in these waters, called Mirabello Bay. However, at the north end of the bay where Plaka is located there are strong winds that can pick up unpredictably. When I previously wrote that the northern cove of Hersonissos had the most protected swim on the north coast of Crete, it was because the Plaka area, even though it appears equally protected, nevertheless has some strong winds that come and go, adding greater risk to the swimmer.

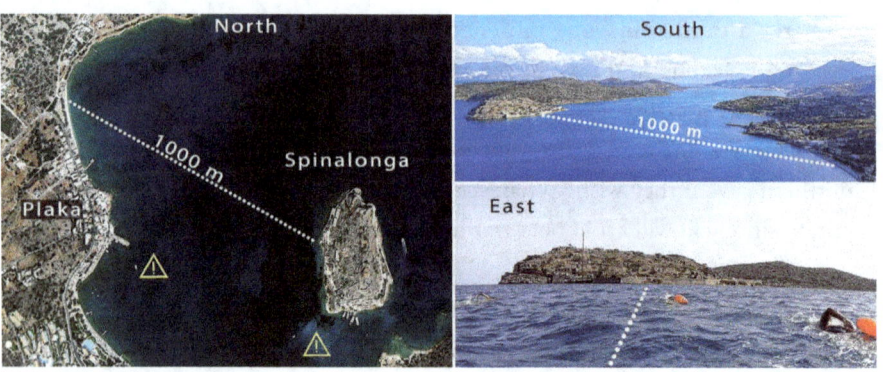

The entry point for Artemisia's Swim is at the northernmost beach (35°18'07.1"N 25°43'36.6"E) of the northernmost village of Plaka. From Agios Nikolaos, one drives north past Elounda and passes through Plaka, arriving at a dirt parking lot along the shoreline. If you drive any further than that, the road curves left, and you will start ascending the mountain.

The swim is 1 km east-southeast from the beach (which has large, rounded rocks) to the Venetian fortress which in recent history (1903–1957) served as a leper colony. The allure of Artemisia's Swim is that you can exit the water at a low, unused pier on Spinalonga (35°17'52.9"N 25°44'12.2"E), and if you are properly prepared with light shoes and clothing you can enter to tour the grounds.

As noted in Chapter 1, Spinalonga is featured in the 2005 novel *The Island* by Victoria Hislop and the location of the 2010 television series *To Nisi*, which is Greek for "The Island." Hislop writes that the distance to the island is a "500-metre journey" when in fact it is no less than 700 m. The swim may be a bit farther than what the book mentions, but the experience of Artemisia's Swim is greatly enriched by having a wonderful novel to go along with it.

The reason to choose the northernmost beach of Plaka is that there are many tour boats doing exactly the same crossing from small piers just south of this swimmer's launch point. These boats travel to the southern tip of Spinalonga, where there is an official entrance gate with a ticket office.

Our swimming destination is a different entrance on the western shore of the island, which on a map of the fortress is marked as the "Garrison room." Visually it looks like an arched entrance through the fortified walls with a few trees in front. There should be no confusion since there are no other arched entrances to be seen. The water becomes shallow near the relatively low pier so that it is easy to step onto the pier on its right side as you approach, taking care to avoid sea urchins.

Just to be clear, even though I am choosing the course with the least boat traffic, you will still encounter some and **a swim buoy is highly recommended.** Remember to stop swimming and **lift your buoy above the water** until you are certain an approaching boat has seen you. The other reason to use a buoy is to store several things needed to enter the site. First, you need some form of clothing since the official rules prohibit walking around in just a swimsuit. Second, you need money to pay the entrance fee, unless it happens to be one of the free days throughout the year. Third, some light footwear will help.

Once you exit the water, you are free to rest on the pier as long as you like without any of the extra clothing mentioned above. However, if you want to enter the fortress by walking through the arch, a guard may greet you and escort you to the ticket office at the south gate to pay the entrance fee. Currently, you can buy tickets online (eticket.tap.gr) to visit Knossos and the Heraklion Archaeological Museum, but *not* Spinalonga. If the guard says they are alone and cannot escort you, then ask them to call a second guard to escort you to the ticket office. If you are with a group of swimmers, I believe the guard would allow one person to get the tickets for everyone while they wait with the guard. I was surprised on one occasion, which was one of the free admission days during the year (none occur in June–August), when the guard still wanted me to get a ticket, just because the rules say everyone needs a ticket. There have also been times when no guard is present.

Another option is to swim an additional 200 m south along Spinalonga's western shoreline to the main entrance ("Dante's Gate") where the boats dock. **Exit the water at or before the southwest corner of the island** (do not swim any closer to the boat pier) and then turn the corner on foot in order to enter the south entrance with all the other tourists. This walk will require footwear because the rocks along the shoreline are jagged. After touring the site, one can re-enter the water at the west entrance for the 1-km return swim. Yet another option is for non-swimmers in your party to take a tour boat to Dante's Gate and greet you at the west gate with your ticket, clothes, shoes, and fresh drinking water.

Regardless of the option you choose, just reaching the pier at the west gate *without* going inside the Venetian fortress still makes the swim a memorable experience. One might even contemplate the irony of swimmers trying to *get into* Spinalonga's fortress while the leprosy patients of long ago only hoped to *get out*.

It is important to be mindful that the wind conditions can change every 15 to 30 minutes. Since the swim to Spinalonga is to the east-southeast, and the winds typically come from the west-northwest, you will reach Spinalonga quite fast, but returning to your starting point could become a more challenging endeavor. Gusts usually last around two minutes and you should change your heading *into* the wind during this time so that you are not blown downwind. Circumnavigating the island is NOT recommended because the channel south of the island is narrow (150 m), congested with boats, and has particularly strong wind gusts.

I find the swim fascinating not merely for the pleasure of arriving at the fortress, but also for studying the illusions that make navigation tricky. The starting beach has a north-south orientation, we depart swimming east-southeast, and a northerly wind will typically push us further southward so that we end up on course to the island. Later, as we leave Spinalonga, we will likely sight forward toward the starting beach to the northwest, but the wind will push us southward again, changing our track to due west—right into the boat traffic we were supposed to avoid.

In other words, swimmers may end up drifting off course, arriving south of the beach in an area that has small boat piers. To compensate, one should swim in a direction to the right of the beach (i.e., north of your line of sight to the beach), which does not look like the correct direction at all. It appears you are swimming towards an isolated mountain north of Plaka. Nevertheless, your track will stay on course to the beach assuming a wind-driven current from the north.

Do not panic if you end up off course and in the boat traffic. These are relatively small boats and they can even rescue you in an emergency. You may have to exit the water at a beach south of your entry point and walk back to your starting beach. You can then enjoy dining at one of the seaside tavernas in Plaka, or inland at my great grandparents' villages of Fourni and Louma. In Louma, the homemade pasta and beer at Mavro Provato make for an exceptional gastroswim.

#11 Mochlos Island and Richtis Waterfall

The small coastal village of Mochlos lies 36 km east of Agios Nikolaos and one can swim 230 m from its beach (35°11'04.1"N 25°54'17.8"E) to an island called Psilos ("flea") or Agios Nikolaos (35°11'10.4"N 25°54'22.9"E) that has early-Minoan archaeology dating from 3,000 BCE. Recall from Chapter 1 that the ancient ruins on Mochlos were oriented in the direction of magnetic north at the time they were built, giving rise to the hypothesis that the Minoans had knowledge of magnetic compasses before the ancient Chinese.

Mochlos is exposed to the northwesterlies so you should expect rough water on windy days. On low wind days I have seen people float over to the island on their inflatable mattresses or tubes. The island and the "mainland" used to be connected and now the water is just a few meters deep between the two. Therefore, you may encounter rolling or breaking waves coming from the northwest. On calmer days this area is appealing to snorkelers. The island has a small pier and other places where a swimmer can exit the water barefoot, making sure not to step on any sea urchins. Circumnavigating the island will be a 1-km swim in addition to the 460 m roundtrip from the mainland.

A 40-minute drive east of Mochlos will bring you to Richtis Waterfall, which has a lovely freshwater pool where you can take an invigorating dip. The elegance and harmony of the 20-m high waterfall is astonishing, as enjoyable and picturesque as any waterfall that I've visited on the Hawaiian Islands. The swims at Mochlos and Richtis fit nicely within a day, highlighting the diversity of Crete's environments. In the Richtis Gorge you might find yourself surrounded by butterflies, which are Jersey tiger moths (*Panaxia quadripunctaria*). They look like white-striped tigers sitting still on a branch and then they magically transform into orange butterflies as they take to the air.

There are several options for how to enter and explore the Richtis Gorge. I think the quickest way to see the waterfall so that you have enough time to visit Mochlos too is to navigate to the "Beach of Richti" (35°11'36.6"N 25°59'02.9"E). If you are on the main motorway (E75), you will drive to the village of Exo Mouliana and look carefully for signs pointing to Richtis *Beach* (not *Gorge*). The road that descends from the motorway to the beach is paved, but narrow and bumpy. After parking near the beach and paying a small entrance fee to the gorge, it's a 25-minute walk (1.2 km) uphill to the waterfall on a well-marked path. Though many wear athletic or hiking shoes, I prefer plain beach slippers or sandals because as the path zigzags across the stream I don't have to worry about getting my shoes wet.

#12 Vai Palm Beach

All the way on the northeast side of the island we find Vai, billed as "The largest natural palm forest in Europe…with more than 5,000 palm trees." I know this because the beach has been developed for tourism and they gave me a multilingual information pamphlet when I paid for parking. Indeed, the grounds are carefully tended and with the palm trees growing up from the sand there is practically no difference between Vai and Hawaii, except for the fact that the Cretan palm trees produce dates and not coconuts. Even the word Hawaii, when spoken in Greek, sounds like Ha-Vai.

Fortunately, the region surrounding Vai is probably one of the least developed places in Crete, perhaps because the road between Agios Nikolaos and Sitia is slow and winding. The road straightens as you travel eastward from Sitia, and the arid mountains have that vibe of getting away from it all. I recommend swimming at Vai Beach ([35°15'12.5"N 26°15'54.4"E](#)) because the water is crystal clear, the seafloor is interesting, and one can explore the islets called Peristerovrachoi ("pigeon rocks") that lie 100 m from the north end of the beach or 260 m from the south end. Circumnavigating the islets is 300 m. Swimming 300 m south of Vai will bring you to a pristine sand dune beach.

For a more exclusive, "insider" recommendation, I suggest driving 2 km north to a dirt parking area ([35°15'53.1"N 26°15'46.3"E](#)) on the northern side of the Itanos archaeological site. The road going north after Vai splits and if you stay to the right, you'll end up at the right spot. From there, you have three options. First you can walk 250 m north across sandy dunes to reach Erimoupolis Beach (35°15'58.6"N 26°15'47.3"E). This beach has no facilities of any kind—the exact opposite of Vai Beach—and it's an insider's favorite. You can then swim south 600 m to Itanos Beach (35°15'43.2"N 26°15'50.2"E). As you head around the cape of the Itanos archaeological site, you are actually swimming over parts of the site itself. The second option after parking is to walk south 300 m along the dirt paths that pass *through* the Itanos archaeological site to reach Itanos Beach. From Itanos Beach, it is a 750-m swim south to the islets in front of Vai Beach. The third option is to enter the water at the small beach just in front of the parking area and swim to either Erimoupolis Beach to the left or Itanos Beach to the right.

Another personal recommendation is to drive 10 minutes south of Vai to Crete's premier windsurfing spot, Kouremenos Beach (35°12'23.3"N 26°16'12.1"E). The sports action happens at the south end of this beach. One can stop by and watch some truly talented athletes attempt various windsurfing tricks on the flat water with strong side-onshore winds. The beach has two windsurfing shops that offer both beginners lessons and advanced equipment for rental. The bay is monitored for safety by the shops, and windsurfers who cannot make it back to the beach are rescued by motorboat.

One travel itinerary hint is that you do not necessarily need to take the northern route eastward from Heraklion to Agios Nikolaos, Sitia, and Vai. Instead, every summer I stay at the unique White River Cottages in Makry Gialos on the southeast coast of Crete. From here I can explore the entire southern coastline westward to Ierapetra. The first 17 km from Makry Gialos to Kakkos Bay have many small bays to swim before reaching the long stretches of sandy beaches east of Ierapetra. In about 75 minutes I can also drive from Makry Gialos to Vai, Kato Zakros, or Xerokambos (swim **#13**) on Crete's eastern coastline. Moreover, Makry Gialos and Ierapetra are the departure points for ferries going to Koufonisi and Chrisi, respectively. These satellite islands have beautiful waters and I mention them again in Chapter 5. For a gastroswim, I recommend dining at Metohi south of Vai and Kaliotzina west of Makry Gialos.

4

South Coast of Crete

THE SOUTH COAST IS MORE PRISTINE and less crowded than the north coast. On any given day, the wind can be quite different compared to the north coast, and there are thermal effects that can make one area in the south of Crete very windy compared to an adjacent area. I usually envision the south coast as having gusty offshore winds whipping down the mountains from the north, or westerlies, typically building up during the day. Offshore winds will create flat conditions for the first 100 m away from shore, whereas the westerlies will generate a lot of chop. The rare southerlies will bring significant waves to the coastline. I also think of the spectacular drives when you travel southward from the north coast. Given that I presented the north coast swims from west to east, I will continue now in a clockwise direction around the eastern tip of the island and list the swims from east to west along the south coast. You will now be swimming in the 350,000 square kilometers of water between Crete and the north coast of Africa known as the Libyan Sea.

#13 Xerokambos Falcon Islands

Did you know there is a falcon that comes to Xerokambos every year for summer vacation by flying 9,000 km from Madagascar? Yes, Eleonora's falcon is Crete's most loyal visitor! It arrives in the spring to breed and departs in the fall for its amazing return journey southward over Africa.

When I told my cousin Mihalis Papastefanakis about this, he beamed with pride, and responded in a thick Cretan accent: Δες μπρε πόσα χιλιόμετρα ταξιδεύουν τα γεράκια απ τη Μαδαγασκάρη στον Ξερόκαμπο για να γεννηθούνε τα κοπέλια τους Κρητικόι!! (Look man how many kilometers the falcons travel from Madagascar to Xerokambos for their kids to be born Cretan!!)

Fortunately, open water swimmers have exclusive access to viewing Eleanora's falcon, also known as Mavropetritis or Varvaki, because it nests on three small islands off the seaside town of Xerokambos. This area boasts picturesque sandy coves and the prime destination for most visitors is a beach called Argilos (35°02'18.1"N 26°13'53.3"E) that has a small cliff made of clay. Here you can paint your entire body and face with the greenish-gray substance until you resemble the undead risen from a shallow grave. Then you wash it off by dipping in the sea and your skin will feel alive again.

My proposed swim route is an 800-m crossing from Argilos Beach to the falcon island called Anavatis (35°01'53.3"N 26°14'05.4"E). This will require calm sea and wind conditions, with attention to any currents. Given the crystal-clear water and moderate depth along the crossing, you should stop occasionally to look down at the sea floor and check if you are drifting. The current may push you southwest so that the return northeastward will be more difficult. You might want to practice my 50% effort rule so that you save strength for the return journey.

As you approach Anavatis you will be able to discern tens of falcons flying in circles above it. One world-traveling birdwatcher (birder) that I know gasped with astonishment when I showed him a video clip from my swim—discovering such a high concentration of falcons in one spot is a rare treat! The falcon's namesake is the Sardinian ruler and falconer Eleanor of Arborea who enacted a progressive legal code in 1392 called the *Carta de Logu* which severely punished anyone caught stealing falcon eggs or capturing young falcons.

The southeast side of Anavatis has the tallest cliffs, and you might notice the falcons entering and exiting the many nooks and crannies where they nest. Circumnavigating the island is an additional 600 m. From the northernmost point of the island, you can take a 400-m route straight to the shoreline, sighting towards a low cave. Then you can swim northward 600 m with the coastline to your left for your return to the clay beach. A route that includes circumnavigating Anavatis will total 2.4 km.

A more ambitious swim is visiting all three islands. The crossing from Anavatis to the slightly larger island called Kavallos is 650 m. The sea is deeper and you will not be able to see the bottom during the crossing. A 20-m wide channel separates Kavallos from the smallest island called Kefali. If you completely circumnavigate all three islands to maximize both your swimming and your birding, then this course amounts to 4.3 km. If you choose not to visit the islands at all, you can still enjoy wonderful swims from cove-to-cove in some of the finest turquoise waters that Crete has to offer.

Finally, note that you can drive to Xerokambos using either a northern route from Sitia or a southern route through Ierapetra. The latter offers jaw-dropping views as you descend the mountain to sea level. Even if you arrive using the Sitia route, I recommend ascending the mountain westward for a thrilling high-altitude view of the three islands, the same scene that the falcons enjoy every year as they complete their incredibly long journey from Madagascar and settle down to eat some delicious Cretan food and give birth to their Cretan babies.

#14 The Galactic Night Swim

The Galactic Night Swim does not take place at a specific location. It's a concept; a surreal experience, more than a place. In this swim, we will contemplate the nature of reality, our place in the universe, the eternal questions about consciousness and the spiritual, and our relationship to all living things. Who knew that a swim could do all that for you?

The key is that we will be swimming in near total darkness, yet our senses will be astonished by pinpoints of light shining from the billions of stars in the Milky Way Galaxy above and the thousands of phosphorescent plankton in the water below. The weightlessness and warmth provided by the sea will diminish our attention to our body and free our mind to explore whatever themes it chooses to explore. Years later, we will remember the Galactic Night Swim as a place and time that recharged our soul.

In the northern hemisphere during the summer, the billions of stars in our Galaxy look like a luminescent, patchy cloud stretching upwards from the southern horizon where you will find the constellations Sagittarius and Scorpius. The darker and clearer the skies, the more these billions of stars will "pop" out of the darkness. In fact, the skies of southern Crete are so dark and clear that many people genuinely think that the light from the Galaxy is a cloud in the sky rather than billions of stars at unimaginable distances away from us.

The center of our Galaxy is in Sagittarius, a constellation that represents a half-man, half-horse centaur holding a bow and arrow. To most people it simply looks like a tea kettle. A curved line of stars to the right of Sagittarius makes up the tail and stinger of the constellation Scorpius, the scorpion. The brightest star in Scorpius located at the head of the scorpion is named Antares, or "opponent of Ares." Ares is the Greek word for Mars. Both Antares and Ares have a reddish hue, but for different reasons. Ares (Mars) is a nearby planet in our solar system with a solid surface that is composed of reddish dirt. Antares is a very distant red supergiant star burning its last remaining gas, which will culminate in a spectacular explosion that astronomers call a [supernova](). In the meantime, it's amazing to ponder that when you look towards Sagittarius, you are gazing at the center of our Galaxy which contains a [black hole]()—one of the most incredible phenomena in nature—though we cannot see it directly. The fabric of spacetime surrounding a black hole is so distorted that light can never escape and time itself appears to have no meaning.

As a night swimmer, the heavens will follow you as you dive into the water and thousands of blue-white stars flash in front of your hands and arms. These are bioluminescent plankton that need to be physically disturbed in order to glow. That's why you will see them appear, each for a split second, around your moving arms and legs. The ancient text De Mundo (Περὶ Κόσμου) that was attributed to Aristotle stated, "there are exhalations of fire from the sea" (γίνεται πυρὸς ἐν τῇ θαλάσσῃ), and this could have been an observation of this very same marine bioluminescence. These plankton are probably [dinoflagellates](), which marine biologists refer to as "dinos." Thus, you can tell your friends that you swam with the dinos at night.

While stars create light from the energy of fusing atoms, living organisms manage to do it through biochemistry. How does a dino's flash of light help it? Given that plankton are food for predators, when the food suddenly flashes, this may disturb the predator, or reveal the location of the predator so that it is quickly eaten by yet another predator. It's as if every time a human pulled a carrot out of the ground we received an electric shock, or the carrot communicated to an alien civilization in space that the human should be immediately vaporized. We would definitely stop touching the carrots!

Though plankton shine in the darkness like stars, they wander the seas like planets. Looking up, the ancient Greeks noticed points of light that seemed to move from night to night relative to the other fixed stars. These were named planets because this word means "wanderer." It would take many centuries of scientific inquiry to understand that these planets are very close to Earth, orbiting the Sun, whereas the stars are located at great distances, orbiting the galactic center in Sagittarius. This means that the motion of a planet in the sky can be perceived to move over many nights, while the stars appear to have the same position year after year. Looking down instead of up, the German medical doctor and zoologist Victor Hensen rigorously studied small marine organisms. In 1887 he decided to call them "plankton" because they did not have the means to propel themselves in water. This "floating stuff" wanders the Earth's globe, just like the planets wander the celestial globe.

To get the most out of the Galactic Night Swim, the main ingredient is to swim under very dark conditions. The darker the environment, the brighter and more numerous these flashes will seem to be. The experience can still be pleasant if you are swimming near lights and with the moon in the sky. But if you are away from the major cities and the moon is NOT in the sky, everything above and below the water will seem much more vibrant and astonishing. The flashes may be more numerous several hours after sunset because bioluminescence follows a circadian rhythm that has peak activity around the middle of the night.

The best times to see our Galaxy are when the moon is absent from the sky. Look for dates around the "new moon". The swim should take place at least an hour after sunset for the skies to become very dark. So, if you find that sunset occurs at 8:10 pm, the night swim will begin at around 9:10. An important safety measure is to practice the swim during daylight, paying attention to beach access, water entry, and swimming conditions. As far as the best month to see the bioluminescent plankton, I have encountered them from June to September (I have not sampled other months of the year).

The best place to see both the Galaxy and the bioluminescent plankton is in southern Crete. You can perceive both on the other coasts, as long as you find a relatively dark beach where the southern sky is not blocked by mountains. Overall, though, the southern coastlines are darkest and have great views of the southern sky. The best conditions for the Galactic Night Swim are warm and still evenings, at shallow, sandy beaches with minimal waves. If there is a slight breeze, the entire experience may be unpleasantly cold, and if the beach has difficult ingress and egress, you may end up with injured feet. A wetsuit top and reef shoes will of course help in these situations. Don't forget that clear-lens goggles are best for seeing the lights.

My recommendation is to wade out to chest-deep water and swim 25 m back and forth close to shore without going any significant distance. **As you wade out,**

look behind you to note any visible landmarks on shore. In near-total darkness, disorientation happens very quickly and unexpectedly.

When in a group, swimmers should call out to make sure everyone keeps track of everyone else. At some point, the group should pause the swimming experience and confirm everyone's well-being. If anyone decides to return to shore, even if it's just to grab something quickly and rejoin the group, it's important that they announce it and confirm that it has been heard by others. Otherwise, the group may discover that someone is missing from the water and fear for their safety. Likewise, someone entering the water should announce to the group that they are joining. Remember, the conditions may be so dark that swimmers cannot see each other, and much depends on what one can hear. Overall, the swim is enjoyable if everyone swims in a small area no deeper than chest deep.

Even non-swimmers can wade out to knee-deep water to enjoy the bioluminescent plankton just by waving their hands vigorously underwater. But the real treat is to take shallow dives with a breaststroke or a sculling motion of your hands and witness the bioluminescence in front of your very eyes! Then come to the surface and float on your back, gazing south toward the Galaxy. Next, dip your head back in the water and look back at your feet as you kick underwater to produce fleeting marine constellations of light. This won't be a long or cardiovascular-workout swim. Consider it more of a playful, splashing around for 10–15 minutes type of swim.

If you start feeling cold, you should exit the water quickly. Unlike daytime swimming under the sun, you will not be warming up at all by walking out of the water. Instead, you will continue to be cold until you find a dry towel and get dressed. If your teeth start chattering, you are already overdue for leaving the water and changing into warm clothes.

Here are a few items I have found useful for night swims:

- Clear (non-tinted) goggles or mask for maximum visual acuity.
- Two towels.
- A flashlight (preferably lantern style) so that you can return to the correct spot on the beach and find your belongings in the dark.
- Snacks and water (because the darkest beaches are farther away from civilization).

- A change of clothes.

Which beach would I specifically recommend as an insider for the Galactic Night Swim? I had heard reports of bioluminescent plankton in Arvi, a small village 90 minutes south of Heraklion, which I confirmed when swimming there in mid-August. However, I also had an equally positive experience in terms of darkness and bioluminescent plankton a few days later in Agia Fotini, which is over 100 km to the west, closer to Agios Pavlos and Preveli, and then again in Paleochora which is another 100 km to the west. I can also see the bioluminescent plankton along beaches on the northern coast, but due to light pollution the light from our galaxy is washed out. So, I believe you will enjoy the Galactic Night Swim as long as it is dark (no moon, no light pollution) and with a clear view of the southern sky. I will describe a night swim in Arvi just for the sake of providing details for at least one location.

This area is famous for its bananas, though Arvi itself is not a particularly memorable village. The night swim experience is excellent because the skies are dark, the beaches are sandy and relatively shallow, there is minimal boat traffic, and the environment tends to be warm and humid. Also, the drive from Heraklion down to Arvi is scenic and has historical World War II interest. As you turn right at the village of Amiras for a final descent southward down the mountain to the coastline you can visit a memorial to the hundreds of local civilians killed by Nazi forces in 1943 as a reprisal for guerrilla activity (the [Viannos massacres](#)).

As the road from the mountains finally reaches sea level, it turns to the left (eastward) with the beaches on the right. The night swim beach ([34°59'28.5"N 25°27'05.3"E](#)) is located 100 m *before* arriving at Arvi's small harbor and buildings. The beach is distinguished by a small outcropping into the sea which may have a flagpole with a blue flag on it. From the elevated road you might find some picnic benches, perhaps a small boat used as a planter, and both a ramp and some rough steps descending to the beach. The advantages of this location are the steps to get down to the beach, the ability to park close to the beach on the road, the freshwater shower at the bottom of the steps, the sandy beach and water entry, and the darkness, since the primary illumination will be from the few streetlamps on the road. Enjoy!

#15 Treis Ekklisies Caves

One hour south of Heraklion we find the rugged Asterousia Mountains and a visually thrilling descent down to sea level toward the small village of Treis Ekklisies (TREES ek-lee-SEE-es), which means "three churches" in Greek. The return trip is also beautiful, and I recommend departing Treis Ekklisies about an hour before sunset, heading northward over the mountain to meet the expansive view of the Messara Plain. In addition to the breathtaking drive, you will have the fantastic experience of swimming along an untouched coastline with the mountain slopes soaring above, great underwater visibility, beautiful marine caves, and minimal boat traffic. The swims resemble the Sfakia area to the west, except with fewer boats and people. As a swimmer, you will feel more "on your own" and far from civilization. As you approach Treis Ekklisies by car, my recommended swims begin from two beaches that are located east and west of the village. After these swims, I suggest returning to the main village of Treis Ekklisies and sitting at one of the tavernas with tables right on the sand for a nice meal. At the end of this section, I challenge multi-talented athletes to attempt my Cretan Quadrathlon that is inspired by the amazing geography of this area.

Westward Route: These swims are in the direction of two spectacular caves and I recommend entering the water at a starting beach west of Treis Ekklisies. This involves ascending the road to travel over the cape, and then descending again via a dirt road to the beaches west of the village. The first beautiful beach (Pahia Ammos) is long with dark sand and dotted with trees, but one can drive 300 m farther west to a smaller beach (34°57'04.6"N 25°07'43.6"E) below one of the last houses. If the wind is too strong, or for those who simply want a short excursion, the swim to the right (west) of this beach features picturesque coves along the first 100 m of the coastline. On low-wind days, a much longer 700-m swim westward will reward you with a visit to a huge cave (34°56'51.9"N 25°07'20.6"E). You can continue hugging the coastline for 100 m past this cave to swim through a series of low caverns. The second terrific cave (34°56'23.9"N 25°06'36.3"E) is located an *additional* 1,400 m westward from the first. Visiting both caves and making the return trip amounts to 4,200 m.

Overall, I would rank these as among the best marine caves to visit in all of Crete. They are both large enough to fit at least two small boats. The ceiling of the more distant cave has a large hole on one side that lets in sunlight, illuminating the turquoise water. I also appreciate the added safety of how the difficult swim westward occurs first, and then the westerlies should help push you back on your return to the starting beach.

The bravest swimmers can visit *The Portal* — a dark, narrow cave near the end of the 700-m swim that is sometimes swarming with bats. The entrance is hidden and reveals itself only as you approach what appears to be solid rock in front of you. You will see a tall portal to the right, but without a marine flashlight you will have no idea how deep it goes. Float slowly into it with your head above the water and using a gentle breaststroke. As your eyes slowly dark adapt, keep going a few more strokes. You are now entering something like the black hole at the center of our galaxy that was discussed for the Galactic Night Swim. When you believe you have traveled just 20 m into The Portal turn around and look back at the entrance. It will appear 40 m away, as if time and space are completely distorted. Continue forward slowly for another 20 m and look back again. The cave entrance will appear as a small slit seemingly 100 m away from you. If you do not have a flashlight, there may be hundreds of small bats flying above you in complete silence, using echolocation to avoid hitting the rock and each other. If you do have a flashlight, you will be astonished with a beautiful sight of these elegant and sophisticated aerial mammals navigating three dimensions of space in complete darkness. The Portal is hard to find, so I would suggest swimming westward to the prominent large cave at 700 m distance, then swimming 90 m back (eastward) along the coastline to search for it.

Eastward Route: The eastward swims have something for everyone, from the beginners who can doggie-paddle with their head above the water, to the skilled open water swimmers interested in 4–13 km distances that will transport them to the most beautiful coastline in all of Crete. The starting point is Voidomatis Beach (34°57'21.2"N 25°09'34.5"E), which means "eye of the cow" given the tall and wide marine cave to the left of the beach. The drive to Voidomatis (vo-ee-tho-MA-tees) is on a 1.8-km dirt road that begins as a sharp left (a switchback going east) from the asphalt road 300 m before you encounter the first buildings of Treis Ekklisies. At the switchback you may also see a small sign pointing the way and large trash bins along the side of the main road. I have traveled the dirt road with a small vehicle that is similar to a typical island rental car (e.g., the Toyota Yaris). Four-wheel drive should not be needed as long as you slow down and steer around the occasional rough patches.

Voidomatis Beach is roughly 40 m long, it has no facilities, yet the sand is comfortable enough to lie on with just a towel. The beach itself has caves for shade.

Since these fill up with other people looking for shade, a beach umbrella might be needed, as well as your own water and food. The parking area is above the beach in front of several homes built directly above the marine cave. On the one hand, these homes are an eyesore within the pristine natural environment. On the other hand, from the swimmer's point of view, they provide a prominent landmark for navigating back to the beach.

The descent from the parking area to the beach is down a short rocky path ending in steel steps, which could pose a challenge for people with mobility issues. Note that the beach directly in front of the village of Treis Ekklisies is probably the most accessible in the area.

Since the large, eye-shaped marine cave along the eastern side of Voidomatis Beach is only a 25-m swim, just about everyone can reach it except when there are southerly or southwesterly winds and breaking waves. If you swim 300 m around the cape, you will discover a longer, more isolated beach. If you swim 120 m to the right (west) of Voidomatis, you can explore a deeper and darker cave.

The longest swim is 6.5 km eastward to the extraordinary black sand beach and marble caves of Aspes (34°57'11.9"N 25°12'43.8"E). However, there are many excellent destinations and unforgettable swim experiences at intermediate distances. Which distance you choose will greatly depend on the wind and sea conditions. For the longer excursions you will need to include water and snacks in your swim buoy. Note that a visit to all the beaches and caves between Voidomatis and Aspes took me *seven hours* for the roundtrip journey. This means that the swim should begin early in the day and the batteries of GPS-enabled devices may die before the swim is over.

The main safety concern is if the westerly wind will make it too difficult for you to return to Voidomatis Beach. I recommend swimming out of Voidomatis to the left (east), hugging the coastline, and stopping frequently to float and determine the strength of any current. If you are noticeably drifting you will have to consider that the westerly may become even stronger and challenge your safe return to Voidomatis. It might be best to enjoy the shorter routes that day and use fins to assist in your swimming.

There are too many beaches and caves between Voidomatis and Aspes for me to describe completely, which means that you will enjoy the thrill of discovering many for yourself. I think that the most amazing segment is the 1-km swim between Kaminaki (34°57'13.4"N 25°10'39.8"E) and Sfakidia (34°57'13.7"N 25°11'16.8"E) beaches. This area has a rugged beauty, magnificent geological features, and an extreme isolation that you might remember later as a surreal experience rather than just a swim.

My nickname for Kaminaki Beach is "mini Agiofaraggo" (swim **#16**) because it also lies at the end of a riverbed that twists through the Perivolianos Gorge. Steep cliffs of orange-tinted rock flank the beach which features large pebbles rather than sand. If you cannot swim as far as Kaminaki Beach, there is a cute beach (Agio Pnevma) that lies 1.2 km east of Voidomatis (34°57'16.6"N 25°10'20.4"E).

Sfakidia Beach is a 1-km swim from Kaminaki but you will probably travel a greater distance as you take detours to explore all the small bays and caves along the coastline. Almost half-way to Sfakidia you can swim under a massive stone arch and then rest on a small black-sand beach hidden beyond it. Just before you arrive at Sfakidia you will find a cave shaped like the Greek capital letter delta (Δ). Sfakidia beach has smaller stone pebbles than Kaminaki and is surrounded on all three sides by cliffs of colorful rock. As you rest here you should decide if you can complete the additional 7 km back-and-forth to Aspes, which will require at least two more hours of swimming. Did you bring enough water? How are you feeling? Is there enough time available before sunset? Without an escort boat there are no safety nets, so you must answer these questions accurately. The first 600 m southwestward from Sfakidia has many tall, narrow openings in the rock worth exploring if you have some energy left but cannot swim all the way to Aspes.

If you make it all the way to Aspes you will be rewarded with a series of caves that I think are more impressive than those at Marmara (swim **#20**). Going to Marmara feels like a pleasant day at the zoo, while visiting Aspes is like time-traveling to witness the grandeur of the Jurassic era. Black sand beaches west of the caves will offer you the opportunity to rest in this majestic environment.

Finally, note that your strategy for the long swim to Aspes may not necessarily follow the timeline above. An alternative is to swim directly to Aspes from Voidomatis when your body is least fatigued. This will be a 5-km swim because you are not turning north to visit Kaminaki and Sfakidia beaches. Visiting these beaches can occur on the return journey, providing frequent rest breaks when you feel most fatigued. At the end of this excursion, you should congratulate yourself since you just swam more than 10 km. This makes you a marathon swimmer, a Pheidippides of the sea!

The Cretan Triathlon and Quadrathlon: The traditional swim-bike-run triathlon seems unbalanced because it has one event in the water and two on land. The Cretan Triathlon, on the other hand, is a hypothetical fly-run-swim event that celebrates the human capacity to explore by air, land, and sea. It conjures the mystical allure of a trinity, each part complementing the other, or the legends of Icarus and Daedalus crafting wings to fly away from Crete, the historic run of Pheidippides between Marathon and Athens to deliver a message of victory against all odds, and the three days that Odysseus swam to save his own life so that he could return home to his family.

The Cretan Triathlon could start at the top of the steep Asterousia Mountains 500 m above Treis Ekklisies with paraglider launches (at timed intervals for safety). The competitors could land at a beach either east or west of the town (depending on conditions) and then race on foot to the swimming launch point that I recommended above. The swim course would be the 700-m stretch of coastline shown in my map, or longer.

This triathlon leaves out cycling, but we could add it to make The Cretan Quadrathlon. Once out of the water, athletes could cycle back up the mountain for roughly 6 km back to where they started their flight. On the other hand, races are fun when they begin and end at beaches. The quadrathlon's first event could be the swim, followed by the run near sea level, then cycling up the mountain, and a final flight back down to the beach. This sequence has an appealing chronological symbolism: life on this planet began in water, humans then thrived by walking on land, eventually inventing the wheel to transport them even farther, followed by the penultimate achievement of mastering flight and departing their home world to explore the cosmos.

#16 Agiofaraggo

Agiofaraggo (Ah-yo-FA-ra-go) means "gorge of the saints" and as you hike down the riverbed for 25 minutes between the parking area and the beach, you'll surely agree that there is no better name for this quiet and mystical place. The small church of Saint Anthony was built within the gorge, marking the religious significance of the region. Even if the church had never been built, any nature lover who feels that trees, canyons, and caves are the cathedrals of this planet would conclude that this area has something truly spiritual about it.

As you walk through the gorge, one of the 300 monks that protect the area may be watching you closely, ensuring that you do not litter. Some say that when one monk dies, they are immediately replaced by another from the surrounding monasteries. The monks are so amazingly holy that they are invisible, except when they choose to reveal themselves. The one thing that gives them away is when they speak. Apparently, the physics of invisibility does not prevent sound waves from travelling through air. In Agiofaraggo, the key is to listen carefully to the wind blowing through the canyon—you might hear the invisible monks talking.

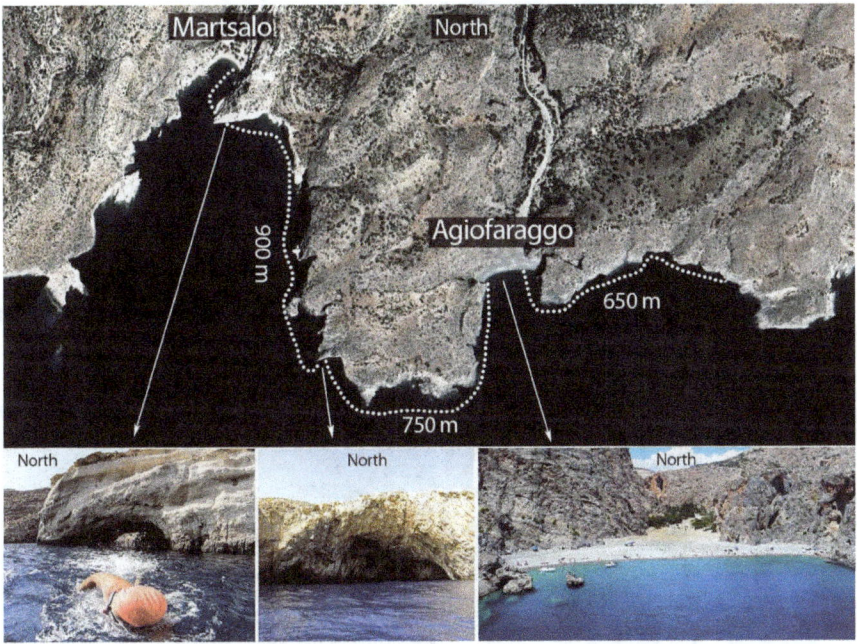

I like the swims to the left and right of Agiofaraggo Beach (34°55'31.4"N 24°46'40.3"E) because the coastline is remote and pocketed with fantastic caves, the water plunges to great depths, creating that visually mesmerizing "deep blue," while the sandy beach itself is remote with *no facilities*. Reaching the parking area to start the hike requires 25 minutes of driving on a dirt road that begins at the

Odigitria Monastery. I recommend navigating first to this monastery, then taking the dirt road going left and following the signs to Agiofaraggo Beach. Make sure to bring your own water and food for the day.

Both the shortest and longest swims that I recommend are to the right (westward), starting from the west side of the beach. Only 20 m from the western edge swimmers can enjoy passing underneath an arch-like rock formation. Swimming 750 m westward around the cape, swimmers encounter a huge cave. The innermost section of the cave may be illuminated by sunlight. At other times you might need a waterproof flashlight. You might also pause to appreciate that you just swam the southernmost route in this book at a latitude of +34°55'20". The African city of Tobruk, Libya—320 km away—is slightly closer than Athens (350 km)! Continuing northward along the coastline for 900 m the swimmer can pass through a cave-tunnel just before reaching the isolated Martsalo Beach ([34°55'47.8"N 24°46'13.9"E](34°55'47.8"N 24°46'13.9"E)). A northwesterly wind will make this final segment of the swim more challenging.

The swim to the left (eastward) of Agiofaraggo Beach also has a series of marine caves. On the map I marked a 650-m swim to an archlike passageway, but there are also several caves to explore at a shorter distance of roughly 400 m.

My personal preference is to visit Agiofaraggo when there is a full moon that can be seen rising if you sit on the west side of the beach. You can depart the beach at night with flashlights to return to the parking area. The canyon is rather spooky in the dark, and you might get a strange feeling that the invisible monks are indeed lurking somewhere nearby, watching you.

#17 Matala's Hidden Sea Caves

The seaside town of Matala is famous for the hippies that came from all over the world to take up residence within the many artificial caves that flank the northern side of its beach. In the evenings it was a magical sight as each cave glowed from small fires and lanterns within. The caves are now unoccupied and have become a mainstream tourist attraction with paid admission, an ironic antithesis to the hippie culture that made them famous in the first place. The town continues to celebrate its hippie identity with funky stores, street art, and an early-summer music festival on the beach. However, Matala is not a favorite spot among open water swimmers because its beach faces west and the bay often suffers from rough water with low visibility.

Fortunately, Matala's sandy Red Beach (Kokkini Ammos) (34°59'13.5"N 24°44'56.6"E) to the south of town is both protected from the northwesterly winds AND has five hidden marine caves to explore. Good footwear is needed to reach Red Beach which is an 800-m hike over an 85-m high rocky hill from an unpaved parking area (34°59'25.7"N 24°44'56.7"E). This is one of the more difficult hikes in the book, yet the views are beautiful along the way. To explore the two deepest sea caves, bring a marine flashlight or a transparent waterproof pouch with a flashlight. The beach has a limited number of sunbeds and umbrellas, as well as some food and drink, but it does not have a fresh-water shower.

My recommended swim starts on the right (northern) side of Red Beach where none of the five caves will be visible at first. After swimming 280 m, you will encounter the first cave with its rectangular opening. The second and third caves are adjacent to each other in a small bay 120 m beyond the first cave. The fourth cave lies just 25 m away from the third, and the fifth is an additional 20-m swim. The fifth cave is unique in that it has two openings along the ceiling that let in sunshine. After the fifth cave, one can swim an additional 1.1 km around the cape to visit Matala Beach. With a typical northwesterly wind this route will be in very rough water, and you may find areas where the current pushes you back towards Red Beach.

The most unique aspect of swimming at Red Beach is to explore the deepest parts of the first and second caves using a flashlight. Shining your light underwater may reveal shrimp along the rocks that live their lives in complete darkness. Pointing the light upwards might unveil tens, or even hundreds of small bats circling in the air silently using echolocation to avoid collisions. You may pause to appreciate how their home world appears pitch-dark to us, but for them countless ultrasonic sound waves serve as innumerable rising suns.

The first cave has a particularly amazing architecture. As you enter the portion that is visible from the outside, you will notice a narrow slit at the back roughly 50 m from the entrance. This is the beginning of a curving hallway that is perhaps 25 m long which leads to a grand bat ballroom that is roughly 10 m wide, 30 m long, and 10 m tall. Don't worry. If the ballroom is full of bats, they will be hanging or flying along the upper parts of the cave and will not swarm near the swimmers. The second cave is narrower and not as deep as the first. Since the ceiling is also lower than the first you can enjoy a closer view of the bats.

Encountering Crete's biological diversity is a real treat for me, but for others floating into dark bat caves where you lose sight of the exit may cause some claustrophobic anxiety. I would recommend moving very slowly and for each person to have their own flashlight. Swimmers should also educate themselves on the potential health risks of exposure to bat guano. Not swallowing water and having healthy skin are important here, as with every open water swim. Even though bat guano must be there, I did not see or smell it in the water and felt healthy after every visit to Crete's marine bat caves.

Whether or not you braved my proposed deep cave exploration, a perfect way to end this swimming excursion is to enjoy the Cretan sunset from either Red Beach or Matala Beach.

#18 Agios Pavlos Full Moon Swim

Agios Pavlos (Saint Paul) is a protected, relatively small, south-facing bay ([35°06'10.9"N 24°33'49.0"E](#)) between Preveli and Agia Galini. Some say that Saint Paul lived here for five months after being shipwrecked on his way to Rome and couldn't leave until his vessel was repaired. One might imagine he enjoyed a swim every now and then in this very same bay, perhaps pausing in the early evening to marvel at the full moon rising over the eastern horizon. A small cave and church of St. Paul can be visited by walking up a series of steep steps that begin 100 m before arriving at the beach taverna on the west side of the bay.

High along both the western and eastern rims of the bay one can find beautiful, scenic walks. If you choose a path on the east side of the bay, looking west across the bay you see Cape Melissa (Bumble Bee), which has the appearance of a "sleeping dragon," as the locals like to say. Cape Melissa has impressive sand dunes that drop down to a long, west-facing beach that is exposed to the typical northwesterlies, and the water tends to be rough, often with breaking waves.

The bay, on the other hand, is protected by the cape and has an interesting cave-arch rock formation (35°06'04.3"N 24°33'47.5"E) as you swim out 200 m to the right. This cave-arch is the mouth of the dragon, and it can also be approached by walking to the top of the cape and descending into it (there's an opening from the sea as well as from land). The threat from watercraft is low, and the beach has many amenities such as a restaurant, showers, and rental beach chairs and umbrellas. You could also swim eastward out of the bay for 600 m where the last 100 m has a towering rock cliff above the swimmer that plunges straight down into the dark blue depths of the sea. If you are skilled at rock climbing, this might be a great spot to practice deep-water soloing.

From the cave-arch you can swim an additional 800 m westward around Cape Melissa to reach the sand dunes beach. For a counterclockwise route, you can walk up and over the cape, descend the sand dunes, and then swim westward with the coastline on your left until you arrive back in the bay of Agios Pavlos. The rugged, rocky coastline features a deep marine cave at the tip of Cape Melissa, though it may be dangerous to approach closely if the sea is too rough. Swimming clockwise around the cape from the bay to the sand dunes might be more difficult against the northwesterlies.

The clockwise route could be transformed into a fun **swim-run race course**. The swimmers would enter from the bay, swim around the cape, then leave the water and run 100 m up the sand dune to arrive at a finish line at the top. This swim-run circuit could be made multiple times in a row, or as a two-person relay. The first person starts in the bay, goes clockwise around the cape, and runs up the sand dune, tagging their partner who must run down the sand dune and swim back to the bay counterclockwise. The first swimmer can walk eastward back down to the bay, hydrate, stretch, and wait to be tagged when their partner arrives so that they have to swim-run a second time. For a 3 km swim effort per person, this would repeat three times.

The first note of caution is that the dunes are made of black sand which becomes extremely hot in the middle of the day during the summer. I personally enjoy the course 90 minutes before sunset which illuminates the dunes with a fiery red. The second is that I have found lionfish lurking in these waters. They were minding their own business in the shadows, but it is important to know that these are venomous if you handle them or collide with them accidentally. However, they tend to lie at 2–3 meters depth and a swimmer near the surface would not encounter them. They are rather interesting fish to look at with their spiny appendages that fan out like peacock or turkey feathers.

The cave-arch rock formation on the west side of the protected bay faces east so that when the full moon is rising the cave-arch is fully illuminated by moonlight. To prepare for a night swim, one should explore both the cave-arch and the water entry points during the day. Many parts of the beach have slippery, shallow rocky surfaces that you should become familiar with. As you start your swim at night, look behind you occasionally and take note of where you entered the water with respect to the lights of the restaurant on the west side of the beach. When you are swimming, look closely in front of you underwater (without diving) to see if your hands are stirring up sparkling bioluminescent plankton. Though it may seem that the air bubbles produced by your hands entering the water are illuminated by the moon, you might notice that some bubbles are more like "sparkles" and these are in fact plankton. Once you reach the cave-like formation you can linger in the water and enjoy your peaceful moon tanning before heading back to the beach. Note that the moon absorbs more than 99% of incident solar ultraviolet light, which means that it has a very high sun protection factor (SPF > 100). Thank you moon!

Do NOT dive deep underwater given the possibility of encountering the lionfish. Stay near the surface with shallow dives. You should return to the beach if you start shivering and find your teeth chattering due to the colder environment. Non-swimmers can enjoy the full moon rising from the western side of the bay, such as from the taverna on the beach.

#19 The Amazing Gorge Swims

Two of the most magical and perhaps completely unexpected swims on Crete are in the fresh water of the Kourtaliotiko Gorge and Preveli. Though Preveli Beach, with its green river surrounded by palm trees, is one of the most famous tourist destinations on Crete, the Kourtaliotiko Gorge to the north of it has a spectacular swim as well. Both require substantial climbing over rocks or up and down steps and the Kourtaliotiko Gorge may require an entrance ticket.

For the breathtaking [Kourtaliotiko Gorge](#) swim, one parks and then walks toward the stone arch with a cross on top—it is visible from the main road ([35°11'43.1"N 24°27'52.3"E](#)). Passing under the arch, one descends 145 steps and encounters a crossroad. To the left, the steps continue to Saint Nikolas Church where one continues walking to view the top of the waterfalls. To the right, another 245 steps descend to a point downstream of the waterfall. After the steps end, there is a short but difficult climb in the upstream direction over or around a rocky outcropping that needs to be taken slowly and carefully. One finally arrives at a pool in front of a narrow gorge and swims some 50 m upstream to the base of the waterfall.

This is an unbelievable experience as the cold, fresh water falls into the narrow ravine from high above on both sides with beams of sunlight piercing the spray if you arrive mid-day. As you advance closer to the large waterfall, you might need to swim more vigorously against the current, or just stand on the pebbly bottom whenever you like.

Preveli Beach (35°09'08.6"N 24°28'23.6"E) is a major tourist attraction because a lush river flows from the gorge towards the sea. The standard way to reach Preveli is from the west where there is an organized parking area located at a substantial height above the beach. From there, one walks down a steep, windy path to reach the beach. I would estimate this is equivalent to 400 steps. However, the walk to Preveli's beach is much less strenuous if you approach from the east. Essentially you would have to take advantage of something like Google maps to figure out all the turns on the small roads to get to the eastern side of Preveli. However, do not insert "Preveli Beach" as your destination because that will most likely guide you to the western parking lot. Instead, your destination should be "Dionyssos Tavern" or "Dionyssos Beach" (35°09'13.1"N 24°28'41.3"E). Once you arrive at Dionyssos Beach, park your car and head west on foot, looking for the path that ascends and hugs the coastline, until you reach Preveli Beach 300 m away. This scenic path is fairly easy and can be done with beach slippers. Preveli has a cantina with water and food, and the trees provide shade, so you just need to bring along beach towels and money.

To explore the river, most people walk along the footpath upstream. For the swimmer, one can enter the water at the base of the river near the beach and then swim for roughly 350 m until large boulders are encountered. However, the water level may be too low for a swim if the winter season lacked snow, or if you arrive in late summer or fall. For a sea swim from Preveli Beach, I recommend going to the left (eastward) for 250 m towards Dionyssos Beach. Along the way you can pass through a fun tunnel where you enter one cave and exit the other.

Note that Agios Pavlos is also relatively close to the eastern entrance of Preveli (45-minute, 19-km drive). Departing Agios Pavlos, search for a GPS route towards Agia Fotini, and then navigate from Agia Fotini a short distance further west to Dionyssos Beach.

#20 Sfakia, Ilingas, Sweet Water, Loutro, Marmara, Talos

If you were to ask me to choose the ONE PLACE to swim out of all the locations in this book, I would tell you, "Go south to Sfakia (a.k.a. Hora Sfakion)." Traveling westward from Sfakia, you will find wonderful swims at Ilingas, Sweet Water, Loutro, and Marmara, plus two more swims just east of the town, one of which I call "Head of Talos Cave."

This entire area is characterized by rugged and pristine mountains, not to mention the cold fresh water that percolates from the ground and mixes with the sea water. The scenic road from the north coast southward to Sfakia is worth the trip by itself, even if swimming is not on your agenda. You will also see plenty of hikers given that the famous Samaria Gorge is located to the west. The ferry that takes passengers from Sfakia to Loutro continues to Agia Roumeli which is where hikers walking southward down the gorge finish their journey.

On top of all of that, this region of the Mediterranean is home to sperm whales. Friends of mine have seen them surfacing just 400 m from the coastline. Whales live permanently here (they don't leave to migrate) because of the deep water and plentiful food supply. The Samaria Gorge plunges into the sea so that when it rains, nutrients are delivered to great depths, sustaining the creatures (e.g., squid) that the whales feast on. Personally, I have only seen a sea turtle meandering around the bay of Loutro, but this was still a delight.

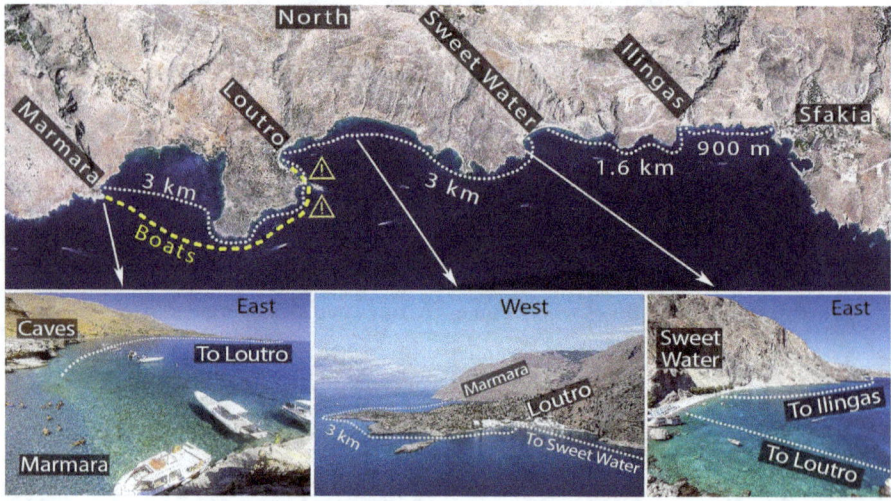

Overnight accommodations are generally available either in Sfakia or in Loutro, though there is free camping (not organized) at Sweet Water. One can drive to Sfakia and Ilingas, but the other destinations require either a hike, kayak, taxi boat, ferry boat or swimming. One common itinerary is to drive to Sfakia, park at the harbor, take a ferry boat to Loutro, find overnight accommodations in Loutro, and then swim to beaches such as Marmara and Sweet Water.

The map highlights the longer swim routes that are suitable (depending on conditions) for stronger open water swimmers, such as those who regularly swim 10 km or more per week. However, swimmers of all abilities can have wonderful experiences by venturing shorter distances away from each beach.

Sfakia (sfa-KYA): You can make your home base Sfakia if you wish, especially since the hotel room rates and food are cheaper compared to Loutro. Or you may find that all the rooms are booked in Loutro so that Sfakia becomes your base out of necessity. Day trips to Sfakia from other parts of Crete are also feasible.

Sfakia and Loutro are connected by a large ferry and many smaller "water taxis" which post their timetables and cell phone numbers around Sfakia's two ports. Sfakia has a relatively large port on the southeast side of town (you will also find a diving center there) and a smaller port northwest of that which is lined with tavernas facing the water. You can walk between the two ports in roughly 15 minutes. The larger ferries to Agia Roumeli and the island of Gavdos depart from the large port, and the smaller water taxis from the small port. In July and August, you should expect to find frequent departures, and if these are not convenient, you can ask around to find a person who has a water taxi service.

My routine is to arrive in Sfakia at 12:30 pm to catch the 1:00 pm large ferry (https://anendyk.gr/) to Loutro departing from the large port. The area in and around Sfakia's port requires a fee for daily parking, but parking farther away from the village along the road is free.

The northernmost side of Sfakia has Vrisi Beach ([35°12'07.7"N 24°08'03.6"E](https://anendyk.gr/)) where one can enter the water and swim westward towards Ilingas beach 900 m away with caves along the route. The best cave experience is actually 100 m east of Ilingas, so I will describe that separately below using Ilingas as the starting point.

Ilingas (EE-ling-as): As you descend the mountain by car and reach sea level, you will begin entering the village of Sfakia and ultimately encounter a parking area (fee required) where you will see a post office, tavernas, bakeries, ATM machines, stores, etc. Roughly 100 m before the town parking, the road has a fork that allows you to turn right, passing a church on the right, and this will take you to Ilingas Beach. You might see cars parked on the left because parking along this side of the road is free. Keep driving and keep an eye out for a sign on the left for a straight driveway that descends to Ilingas.

Ilingas has a taverna where you can park and then walk another 100 m down to the beach ([35°12'08.3"N 24°07'30.3"E](https://anendyk.gr/)). The beach has a small cave-bar with refreshments and snacks. There is also a freshwater shower, but no changing rooms. For toilets, you will have to climb back up to the taverna. The beach has chairs and umbrellas for a fee, but it is worth walking another 100 m to the eastern side of the beach where you can find plenty of shade by putting your towels down on the sand within the towering, double-opening cave facing the sea.

My favorite experience of the entire area is to swim 100 m east (towards the direction of Sfakia) to explore the neighboring beach which can only be accessed from the sea. The eastern side of this beach has a tall cave. You exit the water, head straight back into the depths of this cave, and find a hidden passageway that drops a few meters down a sandy slope into the water and caverns of the neighboring coves. I could describe the entire experience in greater detail, but part of the magic is to discover it all for yourself. The key is to search for the hidden passageway that cannot be spotted unless you walk into the cave. A flashlight is probably not necessary for the experience.

From this beach, you can continue swimming eastward to other caves accessible only to swimmers, including one with a short tunnel connecting two of the caves. If you keep swimming eastward, you will reach Sfakia's northern beach (Vrisi) mentioned in the previous section, some 900 m from Ilingas Beach. Compared to the other swims, the coastline between Sfakia and Ilingas is more exposed to the prevailing westerlies and you might find rougher water. Caution is required as the waves will be travelling straight into the swimming caves.

From Ilingas Beach, you can also swim westward towards Sweet Water Beach about 1.6 km away. A tall, narrow, and deep cave is located 550 m along the coastline from Ilingas. It has a recessed interior space that receives very little light. Continuing the swim westward, one encounters spectacularly deep water plunging straight downward from the coastline. This is a perfect example of the "deep blue" that makes Greece so famous. Finally, note that with the prevailing westerlies, swimming to Sweet Water will be strenuous against the wind and waves, but the return to Ilingas will be easier.

Sweet Water Beach or Glyka Nera (glee-KA ne-RA): The fresh mountain water percolating up from the ground both within the salt water and on the beach itself ([35°12'06.0"N 24°06'26.0"E](#)) is what gives us the "sweet" in Sweet Water. As you encounter pockets of this water while swimming you will no doubt be inclined to call it "amazingly cold water" and not just sweet. The isolation of the beach due to the soaring mountain behind it creates a magical feeling of finding yourself enjoying a pristine spot on our planet. Everyone I have taken to Sweet Water, even those from other Greek islands that are beautiful in their own right, have never forgotten the day that they swam at Sweet Water.

There is no road to Sweet Water. Instead, the vast majority of visitors arrive by water taxi boats that depart from Sfakia or Loutro. Kayakers and hikers can also travel there from Sfakia or Loutro. This is a popular spot on weekends for people with their own small craft to anchor just off the beach. Swimming to Sweet Water is a fairly challenging trek either from Loutro located to the west or from Ilingas or Sfakia to the east.

Sweet Water has chairs and umbrellas for a fee, but there are also trees for shade lining the back of the beach. You might also find a freshwater shower rigged on the beach, tapping into the natural spring wells. For food and drink, there is a small cantina built on a large rock outcropping on the west side of the beach and a basic toilet area behind that. The cantina is where the water taxis dock.

I usually swim to Sweet Water from Loutro, which is a 6 km roundtrip journey. With some coins in my swimsuit pocket or swim buoy I can buy water (and food) when I arrive at Sweet Water. If you wish to make this a one-way 3-km swim, you can purchase your return journey on one of the boats. Swimming 50 m or less from the shoreline between Loutro and Sweet Water will help keep you away from the boat traffic. There are two isolated beaches at about 1.8 and 2.2 km distance from Loutro that you can use to rest.

The tricky thing about this swim is that with the prevailing westerlies you will reach Sweet Water from Loutro much faster and less tired than you may have expected. But then you must swim back to Loutro against the wind and waves. I have found the westerlies pick up in the early afternoon, so you may in fact encounter ever increasing difficulty in returning to Loutro in the afternoon.

For the return trip back to Loutro from Sweet Water, you can try the following:

- PAY ATTENTION to changes in the wind during the day, check forecasts, or ask someone local.
- Be patient with your return swim; lower your expectations as to the speed of the return trip and be mentally prepared for a 50% longer time in the water.
- Take more frequent breaks in the water, and rest at the beaches 800 and 1200 m from Sweet Water.
- Bring enough money to take a water taxi back from Sweet Water.
- Bring footwear in your buoy so that you can walk back for roughly one hour along the hiking trail. Swimmers can access the trail from Sweet Water near the cantina or from the two isolated beaches mentioned above.
- Flag down one of the water taxis for help if you need assistance.

Loutro (lou-TRO): Situated in a cozy bay along the eastern coastline of Cape Mouri, Loutro is well-protected from strong northwesterly winds. Loutro consists of roughly 120 m of beach characterized by smooth round rocks the size of your fist. The main beach (35°11'57.9"N 24°04'43.4"E) is packed with umbrellas and chairs, and during the high season and weekends the entire place can be a bit too crowded. However, the water of the bay is deep and beautiful for swimming and from Loutro one can access the neighboring beaches by hiking, kayaking, swimming, or water taxi.

The large ferry, water taxis, and private craft travel in and out of the bay frequently, so swimmers should generally stick to routes hugging the coastline. Even so, swimmers should keep an eye out for the approach of the large ferry and other craft, particularly if they are swimming in the southwestern half of the bay. Jet skis are rarely present, but the boat traffic may be unsettling to many swimmers. I suggest pausing frequently to scan the surroundings and swimming with a buoy.

Short swims from the northernmost beach where you can hug the northern coastline will keep you far away from the boat traffic. Another relatively short swim is to the islet on the southeast side of the bay. This is roughly 400 m from Loutro's main beach or 100 m from a more secluded water entry point (35°11'50.9"N 24°04'49.7"E) south of the large ferry docking area. The swim from the main beach crosses the path of the large ferry when it is departing or arriving, so make sure you time the swim when the ferry is not approaching or departing the dock. One can check the posted time schedule, or just keep an eye out for it—it is large and slow enough that you should have 10 minutes or more to swim out of its way.

Note that there is only a 50-m gap between the islet and the mainland, and this gap is used by the water taxis going back and forth to Marmara. Therefore, swimmers should never linger in the middle of this gap. You should either be swimming 10 m or less from the mainland's coastline, or 10 m or less from the islet's coastline. If you cross the gap, pay attention to possible approaching small craft and do not stop swimming until you reach the other side.

Circumnavigating the islet is an additional 400 m. The distances are deceiving because the islet is oblong in shape, with the pointy end facing Loutro's beaches, making the islet look smaller than it really is (Projected Shape Error). Nevertheless, the clarity of the water here and generally in the bay is outstanding and makes for a very pleasurable swim. Since Loutro faces east, the moonrise during full moon is memorable and you might see people going for night swims as well. However, be on the lookout for private craft that sometimes arrive in the bay at night.

The longer swims from Loutro are toward Sweet Water Beach, described above, and Marmara Beach, described below.

Marmara (MAR-ma-ra): The highlights of Marmara Beach (35°11'47.5"N 24°03'29.6"E), which means "marbles" in Greek, are the caves along the coastline. If you swim just 100 m to the left of the beach you will find some spectacular caves to explore. First you must reach Marmara, and this is a 3-km swim (one way) from Loutro. You can also rent kayaks or take a water taxi from Loutro.

For the first kilometer from Loutro, the swimmer should try to stay within 5 to 15 m of the coastline to keep a safe distance away from the water taxis. When you finally swim around the southernmost point of the cape and the marble caves of Marmara are sighted across the bay, one should continue around the cape northward for at least another 100 m and then swim 1.1 km westward across the bay to Marmara. The course will be straight to the white marble caves to the right of the beach. This route should keep you north of the course taken by watercraft, which are heading to the left side of the beach (as you head towards it). If you choose to hug the coastline all the way to Marmara, it becomes a 4-km one-way swim but there are beaches along the way to visit and rest.

Marmara has a taverna above the beach with a scenic view, beach umbrellas and chairs, as well as basic toilet facilities. Aradena Gorge lies behind the beach and it can be explored with some basic footwear. As with Sweet Water, the swimmer could always bring money to pay for food and drink at the taverna, and even take a water taxi back to Loutro after dining. Another is for friends and family to take a water taxi from Loutro to Marmara, carrying the swimmers' belongings, and the swimmers rejoin their group at Marmara by swimming at their own pace. The prevailing westerlies will aid the return swim to Loutro.

East of Sfakia – Head of Talos Cave: Did you know that the island of Crete was protected by a giant robot called Talos? The ancient Greeks imagined that you could take metal and fashion it into a machine of superhuman size and strength.

Talos was made of bronze and had the ability to fly, circling the island three times a day, and throwing rocks at any approaching enemy ships. Yet, every Greek hero has a weakness. Achilles was invincible, except for his heel. Orion was the most incredible hunter ever, and then a scorpion bite killed him. In the summer, as you see the constellation Scorpius rising in the east, Orion is setting in the west. The formidable Talos had a single vein located outside of its body that was eventually pulled out, shutting down the first-ever robot. Yet, if the legend were true, wouldn't it be possible to find the remains of a giant such as Talos somewhere on Crete near the coastline that it was protecting?

Sure enough, after an extensive search, I found the head of Talos gazing south towards Africa. One way to see it for yourself is to drive to a delightful cove east of Sfakia called Plakaki Beach (35°11'39.1"N 24°09'31.4"E) and then swim east for 800 m. One needs to take a short hike from a parking area (35°11'40.1"N 24°09'28.6"E) down to the beach. If the cove is crowded with people, you can walk eastward 150 m along the rocky coastline to the larger, neighboring beach. As you swim east you will pass a small white structure along the shore (Agios Pavlos Church) and 200 m after that you will discover the head of Talos (35°11'45.6"N, 24°09'59.4"E). High above the water, two recessed cavities in the rock resemble giant eyes peering south and the mouth of Talos is a cave you can swim into. There are many other caves to explore, but this one is without a doubt Talos.

The tallest marine cave in the area (35°11'35.9"N 24°08'34.4"E) can be found in the westward direction, 1.6 km from Plakaki Beach towards Sfakia. It is easy to recognize because the back side has collapsed and lets in sunlight. On your way there, visit the west side of Ammoudi Beach (35°11'35.2"N 24°08'47.7"E) where you will find a low cave entrance on the shoreline which leads to a marine cave with an opening to the sea.

Summary: There are many combinations for the swims above that also include fun for the non-swimmers. If you are visiting just for the day, then driving to Ilingas Beach and swimming east towards Sfakia to explore the caves along the coastline is my top recommendation (as long as the winds are not strong westerlies or onshore southerlies). The easiest swims are simply near the shorelines of each beach location. If you are a more god-like swimmer, you could suggest that your friends and family take the ferry from Sfakia to Loutro along with your belongings so that you can swim 5 km to Loutro. Or you could start from Marmara and then swim with the westerlies behind your back roughly 8 km to Sfakia. Your friends could even rent a kayak or motorboat as a support vessel. I think staying two nights or more in Loutro is probably the best way to enjoy the region and unwind, though some people may find Loutro too crowded or claustrophobic. Nevertheless, the surrounding mountains, deep blue waters of the bay, and the absence of cars make visiting Loutro a unique experience.

#21 Elafonisi Eye Candy

Elafonisi (Deer or Pirate Booty Island) is one of the several beach destinations in Crete where white-brown-pink sand, shallow water, and crystal-clear turquoise water might make you think you were swimming in the Caribbean or some Pacific atoll. Other similar places are Balos Beach northwest of Chania and two islands off the coast from Ierapetra called Chrisi and Koufonisi. Shallow-water swims have warmer water, but the sandy bottom is not particularly exciting to swim over. I would say that Elafonisi is beautiful to explore and photograph when you are on the beaches, and the swimming is sort of a side dish.

The eye candy attracts huge crowds, but the swimmer can get away from most of it by walking westward past all the beach chairs and umbrellas and wading in waist-deep water across a sand bar to the island (35°16'10.9"N 23°32'12.8"E).

It would help if you brought your own umbrella to plant in the sand. Another way to avoid the crowds is to arrive in the late afternoon, and certainly the redder colors of a setting sun will make the place all the more magical. The southern side of the island has sandy access points, but the northern coastline is rugged and rocky. The farther west you walk the fewer people you will find. One can walk barefoot from east to west along the southern shore for roughly 1 km.

If you enter the water from the eastern side of the island, looking south across the water you will see a low islet called Prasonisi (Green Island) that is 400 m away. The swim is over relatively shallow water with a rocky bottom in much of the area. If you choose your water entry on the west side of the island, then reaching Prasonisi is 1080 m. Circumnavigating the islet is roughly 230 m. One can also enjoy a swim-walk or swim-run clockwise loop by swimming 400 m to Prasonisi from the easternmost beach, rounding the islet, then heading west for 1080 m towards the westernmost beach, and finally travelling on foot 1 km back to the easternmost beach (this works in the counterclockwise direction too).

5

Other Beaches, Satellite Islands & Day Trips

CRETE HAS MANY MORE BEAUTIFUL LOCATIONS for swimming that I have yet to mention. As an encore to the previous two chapters, I will briefly take you on one more clockwise tour of Crete to introduce a few additional swim spots, as well as offering ideas for short excursions away from Crete.

Starting from the northwest coast of Crete, the long stretch of beach at Falasarna (**#22**) is sandy and has a shallow water entry, offering swimming-pool-like conditions on calm days and fun breaking waves on other days. Scuba divers often go on "wreck dives" and here at Falasarna, swimmers can go on a "**wreck swim**" just like at Gramvousa Beach in Chapter 3. One drives northwest towards Ancient Falasarna, enters the archaeological site, and walks south to a small beach (35°30'34.1"N 23°34'06.5"E). From here, it is a 150-m swim (hugging the coastline on your right) to a World War II shipwreck (35°30'32.1"N 23°34'00.8"E). This lies in relatively shallow water and is easily explored as a swimmer or snorkeler from the surface without diving. According to Dr. Michael James Bendon, this is a Tank Landing Craft Mk1 which in 1941, under the command of John Sutton, was on its way from Souda Bay (near Chania) to the southern coast to evacuate thousands of British, Australian, and New Zealander troops. The ship was sunk by Nazi dive bombers, but Sutton and his crew survived. They were sheltered by the local Cretans for some time but were eventually captured as prisoners of war by the Germans. Note that if the archaeological site is closed and the small beach is inaccessible, then a longer swim to the wreck will be necessary by entering the water at one of the other beaches farther to the south. For example, one of the northernmost beaches (35°30'14.0"N 23°34'36.9"E) at Falasarna is located 1,000 m from the wreck.

Moving eastward from Falasarna along the north coast past Chania and up the Akrotiri Peninsula, on the northeast side there is a small beach at Seitan Limani (**#23**; 35°33'06.8"N 24°11'36.5"E) or Satan's Bay, which is one of the two popular fjord beaches on Crete. The other is called Kalypso Beach (**#28**; 35°10'20.5"N 24°24'00.2"E) on the south coast. A **fjord beach** lies at the end of a narrow inlet which curves such that the open water cannot be seen from the beach. These swims have steep rocks on either side, and though the beaches may be narrow and crowded, they are very photogenic. Seitan Limani and Kalypso Beach are featured on many social media posts. Seitan Limani, in particular, often boasts a vibrant greenish water that many find astonishing.

For the swimmer, a key concern is that once you exit the inlet and encounter open water, one cannot look back and see the beach. Therefore, you may become disoriented and not know how to return, particularly when other inlets exist nearby, and they all look very similar. Another major concern is that after exiting the fjord the swimmer may encounter difficult open water conditions that were not evident from the beach.

Seitan Limani (also known as Stefanou Beach) is 16 km north of Marathi Beach (**#2**) and visits to both locations can fit into one day. However, Seitan Limani has the additional challenge of a very steep and difficult hike from the parking area down to the beach. A group may wish to split up into those who will stay at Marathi for the day and those who want to spend a few hours at Seitan Limani. I would recommend swimming 150 m out of Seitan Limani and then turning right and going 200 m into the neighboring fjord to the south which is narrower, has steeper rocky faces on both sides, but does not have a beach.

Kalypso Beach (also known as Karavos Beach) is a 50-minute drive (40 km) south of Rethymno, and 17 minutes from the Kourtaliotiko Gorge. The road descends the mountain and enters a hotel of the same name which surrounds the 100-m long fjord. The hotel maintains several nice features such as walking paths around the fjord, ladders to enter and exit the water, and sunbeds on terraces.

If you are traveling on the northern motorway E75 between Chania and Rethymno, and you enjoy swimming in lakes, then I would recommend a short detour towards Lake Kournas (**#24**; 35°19'56.5"N 24°16'45.1"E). The lake measures roughly 800 m in diameter and renting pedal boats is very popular. Kayaks and SUPs are also available. Afterwards, I make this a gastroswim by dining at the tavernas along the shoreline with views of the water and soaring mountains in the background. Some will be serving delicious lamb antikristo (see swim **#3**).

Crete has several satellite islands that can be visited by ferries or by joining organized day trips. Just north of Heraklion lies Dia (**#25**) with its beautiful deep waters that can be reached by sailing excursions and other small craft. On the southeast side of Crete, we find the islands of Koufonisi (**#26**) and Chrisi (**#27**), with tropical-like, blue-green waters and ferries departing from Makry Gialos and Ierapetra, respectively. The "ferry" from Makry Gialos is outfitted to look like a pirate ship, anchoring at different beaches around Koufonisi (depending on hourly weather conditions) and providing food, drink, and music on board. Gavdos (**#29**) is a permanently inhabited island south of Crete with boats and ferries departing from Sfakia in the morning (also from Loutro, Agia Roumeli, Paleochora, and Sougia). Gavdos has a few overnight accommodations while the other three islands do not. Gavdos also lays claim as the southernmost point in all of Europe; it's even farther south than parts of Africa, such as Algiers and Tunis.

Along the southwest coast of Crete, the town of Paleochora (**#30**) offers two of my favorite beaches located to the west and east of town, named Grammeno Beach (35°13'53.5"N 23°38'13.3"E) and Gialiskari Beach (35°14'12.1"N 23°43'10.4"E), respectively. Both are sandy, and the seafloor and coastline are pleasant, but I also like the town of Paleochora for overnight stays. Note that a previously recommended swim at Elafonisi Beach (**#21**) is slightly over an hour drive away from Paleochora.

For hydrothermal swims, I can recommend two beautiful islands to the north of Crete named Santorini and Milos. A **hydrothermal swim** is a combination of volcano tourism and swimming tourism. It involves entering an area where the water is heated by volcanic activity beneath the seafloor that creates a submarine hydrothermal vent. As you are swimming you may suddenly encounter the following clues that you are on top of a volcano:

- You enter a pocket of water that is unusually warm.
- You sense an odor which you may recognize as sulfur if you have ever been to a volcanic area or handled the substance.
- Looking down at the seafloor, you see a discoloration that resembles white ash after burning wood, or yellow patches due to sulfur or other chemical compounds (mineral sediments).
- You find bubbles rising from the seafloor (mostly CO_2).

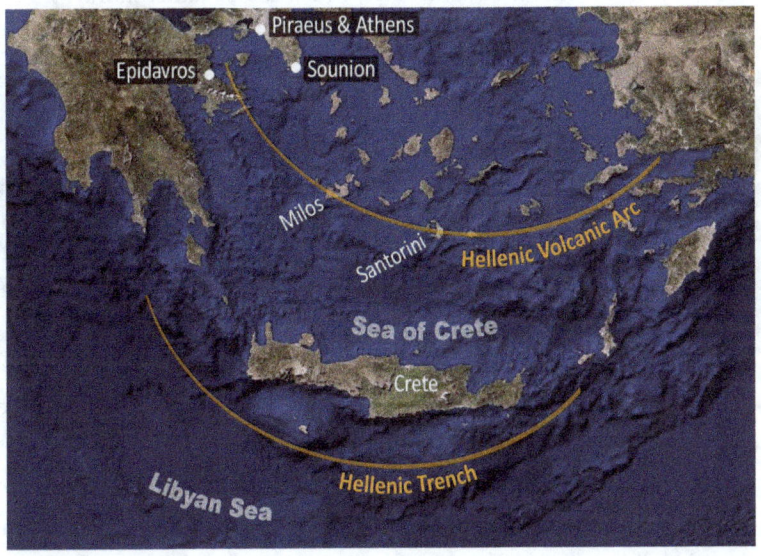

Santorini and Milos lie along the Hellenic Volcanic Arc, which is roughly parallel to the Hellenic Trench off the south coast of Crete. The trench marks where the African tectonic plate plunges northward and downward beneath the Aegean plate. At a depth of 170 km, it begins to melt, creating volcanic activity along an arc north of Crete. This nicely illustrates the Earth's carbon cycle. South of Crete, carbon is a solid in the form of rock. North of Crete, the same carbon rises into the atmosphere as the greenhouse gas CO_2, which helps keep our planet warm enough to be habitable.

Day trips are possible to Santorini using high-speed ferries from Heraklion that depart in the morning and return in the evening. Visiting the island of Milos might require a one-night stay before returning to Crete. Since both Milos and Santorini are located between Crete and Athens, another option is to add extra days to your itinerary and visit them on the journey between Crete and Athens.

The singular allure of Santorini is to walk through the villages of Thira and Oia perched atop the volcanic caldera and enjoy the unforgettable views. These places have global-level eye candy that are uniquely Greek. The middle of the caldera has a hydrothermal swim at the islet of Palea Kameni that can be reached through paid excursions. You would join many other tourists on a boat that stops to allow everyone to enter the warm water, which can be rather murky.

Kleftiko (Milos)　　Hydrothermal swim at Paleochori

Milos has a fantastic hydrothermal swim starting on the west side of Paleochori Beach that features red sea cliffs (36°40'29.9"N 24°30'59.1"E). As you swim westward you will find CO_2 bubbles bursting upwards from the sandy seafloor and the water may have a yellow tint from minerals. Dive to a spot on the seafloor with white ash and place your hand on it to feel the warmth. Continue swimming westward to find a small beach with delightful orange sand and just beyond that a tall boulder on the shoreline surrounded by yellow rock. If you climb out of the water, the rocks will be warm, and you may notice puffs of steam rising from a vent behind the massive boulder.

So, is it worth adding time and cost to your itinerary for a hydrothermal swim? I think the answer has to do with whether you would like to experience other aspects of these islands. Like Santorini's caldera, Milos has a super-photogenic location called "Moon Beach" (Sarakiniko Beach) and hosts a spectacular swim spot called Kleftiko (36°39'02.1"N 24°19'54.7"E) with multiple tunnels and arches. Both islands have places to watch a "famous sunset" and restaurants with great cuisine. However, if you are on a budget, you will probably end up appreciating Crete much more once you see the higher prices on Milos and Santorini.

Finally, my favorite swim over an archaeological site is the "Sunken City" of ancient Epidavros, located about 50 m from shore in water only 1–2 m deep (37°37'32.6"N 23°09'27.1"E). One sees the ruins of a Roman villa with walls, floors, and round cisterns over an area 40 x 15 m. Be careful. Stepping on the ruins or touching anything is forbidden. Even though this is a short swim, the trip is worthwhile because it is a truly unique experience and the ancient amphitheater of Epidavros (a short drive inland) is one of the most amazing archaeological sites in Greece. Thousands of years ago this open-air theater seated 14,000 spectators who watched performances of music and drama. The architects and engineers designed the amphitheater and its limestone seats so that a voice on stage can be heard perfectly well even from the very top row. If one stays overnight during the summer, one can watch a live performance as part of the Athens Festival. Next to the amphitheater lies the Temple of Asclepios. Asclepios was the demigod of medicine and visitors from all over the ancient world would come here to sleep in a large room with snakes, where their dreams would reveal their ailments and therapy. Another nearby site is Ancient Mycenae with the imposing palace and burial tomb of King Agamemnon.

I would recommend touring the ancient sites first and then cooling down with a swim at the sunken city later. A day trip from Crete involves flying to Athens first thing in the morning, renting a car, driving 2 hours to Epidavros, spending 5–6 hours at the archaeological sites and beach, and then driving back to Athens to catch the last evening flight back to Crete. Note that traffic is much slower going to Epidavros on Saturday mornings and returning to Athens on Sunday afternoons because the roads are clogged with Athenians on weekend excursions.

A potentially less expensive option is to take an overnight ferry (which can transport your car) from Heraklion or Chania to Piraeus (the port adjacent to Athens), arriving around 7 am. By 10 am you will be visiting the ancient sites, and if you start heading back to Piraeus around 5 pm you should be in time for the overnight ferry back to Crete that departs at 9 pm. One could even squeeze in a quick visit to the magnificent Acropolis and Parthenon in Athens which close at 8 pm and are a 30-minute drive from Piraeus.

Of course, staying overnight near Epidavros in the wonderful city of Nafplio, or in Athens, will make the entire trip more relaxed. If you choose Athens, I recommend a 1-hr drive southeast for a sunset and full-moon swim under the 2,500-year-old Temple of Poseidon at Cape Sounion. The starting beach lies just north of the cape (37°39'16.9"N 24°01'28.2"E). The bay is well-protected from northerly winds and a line of buoys separates a swimming area from the anchored boats. If you would like to join local open water swimmers closer to Athens, check out WeSwim.gr for their free weekly swims as well as special events such as a gastroswim that combine swimming with fine local dining. Yum!

6

Crete Open Water Swim Competitions

GREECE HOSTS MANY OPEN WATER SWIMMING EVENTS on various islands and the mainland. Some may be difficult to find since they are advertised in Greek and are relatively low key. One hint is to look to Facebook for information since many Greeks use that social media platform for announcing social, cultural, and athletic events. Note that a medical certificate of good health may be required to participate in a race.

Perhaps the most famous Greek open water swimmer (demigod status) was Jason Zirganos from the mainland Greek city of Volos who swam the English Channel (34 km) successfully at least four times ('49, '50, '51, '54). In the 1950 event, nine swimmers made it and 15 did not. That year, *Time Magazine* wrote, "Jason Zirganos, 40, Greek army major, decorated by King Paul last year for being the first Greek ever to swim the Channel, who beat his 1949 time by more than two hours." The winner was an Egyptian army lieutenant, Hassan Abd el Rahim, who broke the record with a 10-hour, 53-minute crossing. Another Greek swimmer, Panagiotis Kamberos was attacked by a shark and had to climb aboard a support boat.

Today, Volos hosts an open water swim named after Jason (Iason in Greek) Zirganos with 5, 11, and 29-km courses. If you visit Volos, which was the home base of Jason and the Argonauts, I can highly recommend swimming along the eastern coastline of the Pelion peninsula. The walk down to Fakistra Beach ([39°23'23.7"N 23°11'36.4"E](39°23'23.7"N 23°11'36.4"E)) is particularly stunning.

It was Jason Zirganos along with Spiro Gardelaki who are known to have made the first crossing in the 1950s between Heraklion and Dia—roughly a 11.5-km swim. In 2007, lifeguard instructor Dimitris Klados organized a swim that started at Dia and ended at Karteros Beach (swim **#8**) in honor of his father, who was tragically shot to death. The swim was called "The Minoan Marathon–Dia to Karteros–Kladios Route." It was held in early September and took place up until 2015. Hopefully it will be held again in the future. Swimmers met around 6:30 am at the small port in Heraklion and boarded boats that transported them to Dia. There was a time limit of five hours to complete the swim southward to Karteros. The lead swimmers finished in roughly 3 hours, 40 minutes and the weather conditions were usually 1–2 Beaufort.

Long distance swimmers can attempt a do-it-yourself approach for the Minoan Marathon by contacting Sailing Crete and requesting passage to Dia aboard a sailboat and an escort back to Heraklion. The request should be made at least two days in advance since it needs to be approved by the Port Authority. The swim will likely be authorized with restrictions, such as requiring calm conditions.

A second organized open water swim competition began in 2013 called "Kalydonia" (ΚΑΛΥΔΩΝΙΑ), which is another name for the island of Spinalonga. It also took place in early September and the course was similar to Artemisia's

CRETE SWIM

Swim (swim **#10**). The starting point was at the southern end of Plaka at Mirabello Park, near the Agia Irini church where my grandmother Artemisia is buried. The 1.8-km course was back and forth (east–west) to the middle of Spinalonga, or around the island for the longer 3.0-km course.

Quick tips for open water racing

Competing in open water races offers a wonderful sense of athletic achievement and belonging within a community of like-minded people. I would recommend coming to Crete a few days early and swimming my routes first. This will introduce you to Crete's sea conditions, which may be choppier and saltier than many other places around the world. Swimming these routes will also teach you to sight forward accurately and swim straight, providing a considerable advantage in open water racing. However, be careful about sighting towards buoys because these are probably in the sea for jet skis and other boats, not swimmers.

When you arrive at the race location an important task is to study the course and memorize the following: Which are the turn buoys, as well as the guide (sighting) buoys between the turn buoys, what are their colors and shapes, what are the distances between them, which side of the buoy (to your left or right) are you supposed to swim, at what angle is each change of direction around a turn buoy, and what are the protocols and exact paths for the start and finish? Instructions and maps will only tell a part of the story. Check the buoys yourself and ask questions such as, "Are the turn buoys really the same color? Can I distinguish their shapes clearly from a distance?"

One key tip for successful sighting is to locate a distant and tall landmark behind each race buoy that you are swimming to. The problem for a swimmer in the water is that a buoy can be difficult to spot every time they sight forward. A better target is a tall landmark behind it which will also permit them to sight forward with their head lower in the water and for a shorter amount of time. From the shoreline before the race, you should study the entire horizon and note everything that is tall. When you are swimming the race, you should spend an extra moment sighting the next buoy, identifying a tall landmark behind it, and then continuing the swim by sighting the landmark as a proxy for the buoy. Also, trust yourself. An error I have witnessed at every open water race is swimmers blindly following someone in front of them who is going in the wrong direction.

Another tip is to make a plan for entering and exiting the water quickly. For a beach start, one should run as far as possible through the water until it is near waist high before beginning to swim, and likewise for exiting the water at the finish. The water depth can be checked before the race. You may even learn that the seafloor is rocky instead of sandy and you might prefer swimming over it rather than risking an injury to your foot.

More tips for open water swimming techniques can also be found in Chapter 2. For example, the buoy in front of you forms a transit line with the buoy behind you, which means that sighting backwards will help in swimming straight. The most general tip I can offer is to participate in many different races and pay attention to how each one taught you something new and made you a better swimmer.

Sighting forward through time

You don't have to be a god, demigod, or an [oneironaut](#) (precognitive dreamer) to foresee that the number of competitions and competitors is going to increase manyfold in the future. Open water swimming is said to be one of the fastest growing sports and recreational activities of the present day. The reader can look into [Crete Open Water Swimming](#) on Facebook, [The World Open Water Swimming Association](#), or the [Outdoor Swimming Society](#) to keep up with the latest developments. Even the Summer Olympic Games now feature a 10K open water competition. So, if you find that you are now stronger and faster after swimming my suggested routes around Crete, then, who knows, one day you might transcend the mere mortals like me and become an Olympian!

Glossary

108: The free number to dial for the coast guard.

112: The free number to dial in cases of emergency.

adventure swim: A swimming excursion aimed at exploration and discovery of islands, coastlines, and marine environments.

Asymptotic Curve Error (ACE): When the line of sight to the asymptote of a curved surface is mistakenly interpreted as the corner of a polygon.

bearing: An angle.

Beaufort: A system of categorizing wind conditions; the higher the number the stronger the wind.

call a swim: Cancel or cut short a planned swim.

cave beach: After swimming into a cave, the water becomes shallow and the cave has a beach inside of it that allows the swimmer to exit the water.

CPR: Cardiopulmonary resuscitation for emergency lifesaving taught in First Aid training programs.

CPR Thoughts: Focusing the mind on **C**oping, **P**ower, and **R**eward thoughts to combat anxiety and panic.

course: A swimmer's intended path over the water relative to fixed landmarks.

current: A horizontal motion of water.

drift vector: The speed *and* direction of a ground track for a floating object moved by water current and wind leeway.

ebbing (emptying): When the tide is going out (the water level is lowering).

fix: A position.

flooding (filling): When the tide is coming in (the water level is rising).

gastroswim: An excursion that combines swimming with fine dining.

heading: The direction the body and head are facing in a swim.

Heading Rotation Error (HRE): When the swimmer does not notice that their heading towards a destination is rotating as their track goes off course due to wind and current.

hydrothermal swim: Swimming in places with hydrothermal (volcanic) activity.

knot: A unit of speed, equivalent to 1.852 km/h (1.15 mph).

leeway: The force of wind acting directly on a swimmer.

marine cave: A cave that you swim into rather than walk into.

Mediterranean diet: Eating while in Crete.

meltemi: A seasonal summer wind.

Projected Shape Error (PSE): Incorrectly deducing the three-dimensional size of an object from its one- or two-dimensional appearance.

range: The distance between two points.

RASP: A mnemonic for surviving a rip current. A swimmer should **R**ecognize they are in a rip current, **A**ccept that swimming against the current to shore could lead to drowning, and then **S**wim **P**arallel to the beach to exit the current channel before swimming towards land.

rip current: A relatively narrow channel of water motion from the beach out to sea.

Say cheese, then breathe: A technique to sight forward during freestyle with the eyes looking forward above the water for one second, then turning the head sideways to take a breath.

sighting: Looking above the surface of the water.

stroke cycle: Every time the same hand (e.g., left) enters the water (one stroke from the left and one from the right equals one stroke cycle).

tidal stream: A water current due to tides ebbing or flooding.

tide: The daily increase and decrease of the sea water height.

track: A swimmer's ground path relative to fixed landmarks and the seafloor.

transit line: A line between two fixed landmarks used to assess a swimmer's position or track.

three-buddy problem: A situation where a third swimmer needs to rescue the two swimmers in the two-buddy problem. Solutions are taught in water safety training.

two-buddy problem: The real threat that a drowning swimmer will also drown the person trying to rescue them. A water safety course teaches important lifesaving methods.

Disclaimer

As noted throughout the book, the content reflects the travel opinions and experiences of the author in Crete during the months June to September before 2021. The author is not a trained or otherwise authorized medical doctor, health professional, sports coach, or marine professional. The information provided is anecdotal, it may have unintentional errors and/or omissions, it may become outdated, and it does not sample, quantify, and update differences in conditions from hour-to-hour, day-to-day and year after year at the swimming locations described. Also, there are significant differences in how individuals respond to both physical and psychological challenges at any given moment. Therefore, the author and publisher indefinitely disclaim liability for events and/or outcomes that result from the content of this book, or any derivatives of the content that may appear elsewhere.

Index

accessible water entries, 7, 104
Agia Pelagia, 76
Agiofaraggo, 106–108
Agios Nikolaos, 3, 86, 89–92
Agios Pavlos, 110
Amnisos, 82
ancient, 1, 2, 18, 33, 48, 76, 81–82, 89, 97, 122, 131–132
Antikythera mechanism, 48
anxiety, 39, 54, 72, 137
Argyroupolis, 72–73
Aristotle, 31, 97
Artemisia, 85–87, 134
Arvi, 100
Athens, 4, 108, 130–132

Bali, 75
Balos, 68
bats, 49, 102, 110
Beaufort, 10, 23–25, 28, 46, 75, 134, 137
bilateral breathing, 50, 54–55, 57
bioluminescent plankton, 2, 83, 96–113
birder, 95
blind and visually impaired, 7, 46
Boufos Cave, 83–84
buoy, 10, 14, 29, 41, 45–49, 69–70, 79, 82, 84, 87, 104, 119–120, 135–136

Cape Souda, 78
cave, 5, 7, 41, 73–74, 79–80, 101–104, 111–112, 117–118, 121, 137–138
Chania, 3–4, 48, 67, 70, 73, 123, 126–128, 132
checklist, 33, 62
Coast Guard, 28
compass, 9
competition, 20, 48, 133–136
CPR Thoughts, 40
Cretan Triathlon, 106
current, 11–14, 21–25, 62, 71–72, 89, 137–138

deep blue, 107, 118, 123

Dia, 128
drowning, 27, 31, 34, 38, 42, 50, 53, 139

eggbeater kick, 54
Elafonisi, 67, 123, 128
emergency, 20, 27–28, 37, 40, 48, 62, 65, 89, 137
Epidavros, 131
Erimoupolis, 92
eye candy, 123–124, 130

Falasarna, 3, 126
falcon, 93–95
first aid, 31
fjord beach, 70, 127–128

Galactic Night Swim, 95–100
gastroswim, 72, 89, 92, 128, 132
Gavdos, 74, 117, 128
gorge, 90, 115, 128
Gramvousa, 68
Green Coast, 25, 76–79

Hellenic Volcanic Arc, 129
Heraklion, 4, 23, 48, 67, 75–76, 79–84, 92, 128, 130–134
Homer, 7–8, 13, 81
hospital, 32, 57
hydrothermal swim, 128–130

Ilingas, 115–119, 123
Itanos, 91

jellyfish, 2, 6, 40
jet skis, 29, 30, 34, 82

Kalypso Beach, 127–128
Kamari, 72
Karteros, 81, 134
Knossos, 76, 80–82, 88
Koufonisi, 92, 123, 128
Kourtaliotiko Gorge, 113

Lake Kournas, 128
lifeguard, 29, 31–32, 36, 45–46, 61–62, 82, 134
lionfish, 6, 40, 112–113
Loutro, 115–123, 128

Makry Gialos, 92, 128
Marathi, 18, 67, 70–72, 127
Marmara, 115, 116, 120–123
Matala, 7, 108–110
Milos, 67, 74, 128–130
Minoan, 5, 9, 82, 89, 134
Mochlos, 89
moon, 14–15, 98, 108, 110–113, 121, 132
mountain bike, 76

navigation, 7–22, 33, 43, 54–55, 57, 61–62, 88
night swim, 21, 42, 64, 83–84, 95–100, 112–113

Odysseus, 7, 8, 81, 84
organized swimming tour, 36

Paleochora, 128
Paleokastro, 79
Peninsula Hotel, 77
pharmacies, 32
Plato, 31
Preveli, 100, 110, 113–115
Psaromoura, 77–78

race, 8, 47, 106, 112, 133–136
Rethymno, 3, 48, 67–68, 72, 75, 128
Richtis Waterfall, 90

Samaria Gorge, 115–116
Santorini, 3, 67, 68, 128–130
sea arch, 74
Seitan Limani, 70, 127
Sfakia, 67, 115–123, 128
shipwreck, 68, 70, 126
sighting, 7–14, 18, 50–55, 57, 59, 83, 135–136

Sounion, 132
Spilies, 7, 53, 73–74
Spinalonga, 5, 11, 85–89, 134
Sweet Water, 7, 115–121
swim-run, 112, 124

Talos, 115, 122
tavernas, 70, 79, 89, 101, 117, 128
The Island, 5, 87
tide, 21–22, 137–138
transit line, 17, 19
Treis Ekklisies, 101–106
triathlon, 106
tunnel, 7, 40–41, 53, 55, 63, 73–75, 80, 118
turtle, 5, 116

Vai, 3, 91–92
Venetian, 2, 5, 68, 79, 85–88
Victoria Hislop, 5, 87
visibility, 2, 5, 14, 20, 44, 46, 64, 77, 101
Voidomatis Beach, 103–104

water temperature, 20
waterfall, 90
weather forecast, 24, 33, 36
whale, 6
windsurfing, 92
World War II, 100, 126
wreck swim, 126

Xerokambos, 93
Xerxes I, 86

Zeus, 1, 82
Zirganos, Jason, 133–134
Zorba the Greek, 5, 70

About the Author

DR. PAUL KALAS is an accomplished astronomer who spends his nights seeking out undiscovered planets among the billions of stars in our galaxy, and the days searching our own blue planet for unforgettable swimming experiences. When he sleeps, he dreams about future adventures. He is the book's insider swim guide, having spent a lifetime exploring Crete's pristine waters, along with four generations of family who were open water swimmers around this remarkable Mediterranean island.

www.ingramcontent.com/pod-product-compliance
Lightning Source LLC
Chambersburg PA
CBHW071851070526
44583CB00016B/1635